Escaping Madness

Mark Robinson

Published by STARMAN, 2024.

ESCAPING MADNESS

First edition. April 8, 2024.

ISBN: 979-8224258253

Written by Mark Robinson.

Table of Contents

For Kris

FOREVER FRIENDS

Praise For
Escaping Madness
A Journey to Awakening

If you have wandered this earth thinking why certain things are happening to you repeatedly and for no reason, take a moment and pick up this book! Mark's honest take on his life, loves, religion and health, courses through a remarkable road paved with learnings from fellow travelers who arrived from unlikely places but at the right time. This book is a gift for anyone looking to find themselves in the throes of chaos or just looking to make sense of what's happening around them.

Sylvia Low Tiffany

Literally a page turner. Though this may not be a "typical" (is there such a thing?) journey, the author touched upon our times in very readable, relatable ways and ends with giving us all hope, and for me faith, that if we sit tight, be the light, participate in our lessons (opportunities) all will be well. Escaping Madness encourages me to breathe, continue on my journey, and that my own knowingness is true.

Jane E. Fletcher-Ortman

Join Mark on his unique spiritual journey as he navigates the challenges, opportunities and joys of Earth School! Mark was led from an early age to explore teachings and modalities to assist him and countless others from his early adolescence. Ultimately, he has triumphed by finding fulfillment, happiness and his tribe bringing a deep love for humanity to all who know him.

Patricia Leigh Allen

Forward

I love telling stories. I have a lot of them. One for every occasion. Life for me has been one big spectacular adventure and I fearlessly went along for the ride, allowing it to take me from one amazing experience to another. Things I had never dreamt of doing, but did anyways. Sometimes, it seems to me that the number of stories is endless. In retrospect, I see that it *all* had a purpose and each experience contributed to the greater purpose.

I came into this life with a big heart. My capacity to love is immense. I have the kind of energy, loving and accepting, that puts people at ease and makes them feel safe. People very quickly relax around me and let all their defenses down. Invariably, they feel safe to open up, and they start sharing their stories, their problems, and their challenges with me. When they are done talking, if I can, I lean forward with a big humorous smile and conspiratorially say, "I have a story for that!" I share how something similar happened to me and how I gained from the experience in a positive way, giving it purpose in the hope that it might give insights into whatever they may be dealing with. I like to keep things light and easy. I try not to get too serious. After all, life is an illusion.

I live a life of service. I always try my best to be helpful.

Luckily, I was blessed with the courage, or cluelessness, to be different and live life out of the box. My mother called me willful because I always insisted on doing what I wanted in my own way. I was her feral child always running around naked, much to the neighbor's displeasure. My interests and entertainments were much different than other children my age and I freely expressed them without apology. Of course, that meant I spent a lot of time alone. But, better to be alone than to be or do something that wasn't going to bring me happiness. Instead of cartoons on TV, I went into my own imagination and created a much more loving world than the one I was experiencing. I had a unique style of dress that set me apart. I freely expressed my ideas and opinions to anyone who would listen. I would shrug off any vexation from family or friends. In truth, I didn't care what other people thought of me or my choices. When I was 16, an older sister of a friend of mine observed that I definitely marched to the beat of my own drum, compared to other teenagers. I never thought about it before then, but it was an accurate observation for sure. I lived in my own little world where life was filled with limitless potential. I was oblivious to the norms of society trying to mold me to conform to its standards. I have always been very comfortable being different. I never understood why people all wanted to look and act the same way. Throughout my 20s, I wore a button that said, "WHY BE NORMAL," on my coat jacket or the thigh of my jeans. I reveled in my originality. Diversity is where it's at! Being different gives you a license to be unique, creative, honest, and fun. I always wanted to have fun! I still do. This enabled me to have a life few could even imagine - rich and full, reaching beyond all boundaries. My forays into the world filled my "tool box" with an endless supply of stories to share.

Not that there isn't a price to pay for being different. Society doesn't approve of nonconformists that don't toe the line. It keeps some things out of reach from those who dare to be extraordinary and reserves them for the people who are unconsciously playing the proverbial game. For the young of age being different leaves you open to being bullied, teased, and beat up - speaking from experience. I wish I could say that it stops at a certain age, but it doesn't. There are bullies throughout life. People notice when you don't fit in or you stand out in the crowd. For whatever reason, it makes them uncomfortable. They don't want to be around it. Access to their social circles and job opportunities become closed off to you. Many people end up feeling beat down by life when they are denied the ability to make a fair, honest living. For me, these experiences just added more tools to my toolbox. Tools like acceptance, understanding, appreciation, tolerance, and compassion. The greatest tool of all is to be able to listen *and* hear what is being said, without judgment or presumption.

Now, let's get back to having fun! I don't want to say that I get bored easily, but I will admit to having a short attention span. Luckily, I've always been good at entertaining myself. I like me. I like my company. I enjoy being by myself. But when I'm in the mood for companionship, I do gravitate towards people that are exciting, different, edgy and adventuresome. People who like to push boundaries or ignore them altogether. People like that excite me. I like to think of them as the "Idea" people. Actually, I just described myself, so let me amend my statement to, "I gravitate towards people that are exciting, different, edgy, and adventuresome, like myself". I may like to be alone but it is always more fun to have somebody at your side to enjoy the adventure with. That special someone who dares to see a Keep Out sign as an invitation. It was obvious from an early age that I was a rule breaker and didn't mind being one step on the wrong side of the law. What are rules and laws anyway? My will always seemed to guide me to the experiences I needed, in order to learn and grow. There is something very spiritual about being in the flow; letting one moment take you to the next without thoughts or Keep Out signs to hold you back. I believe this is how a life should be led. Not following the rules leave us open to infinite possibilities.

Before I begin, I want to clarify that I understand my entire life to be a spiritual journey; a succession of opportunities and challenges to learn and grow. Life is dynamic, rather than static. In Anatomy class, I learned that in order to move a finger, all 600 muscles in the body have to adjust in one way or another to make it happen. Life is the same way. Everything that happens will affect everything that has and will happen. You may have questions along the way when reading this book. That is because at the time they happened, I didn't have the answers. They came later as I gleaned new experiences, knowledge and understandings. I promise that by the time you finish with the book, everything will have been answered and clarified. Enjoy the ride!

My goal is always to achieve the best that I possibly can in this life so I will have a more advanced starting point in my next incarnation here on Earth. When we heal our wounds, we leave them behind us and move forward into a higher vibration which will enhance all future incarnations. Once authentic healing occurs, we can only move forward. This understanding came to me through a difficult time in my life. I'll tell you that story later in the book. My hope is that, by example, my healing path will let the reader know that they are not crazy nor alone as they awaken into their own spiritual awareness and give inspiration and courage to choose to go down their own unique path of healing and evolution. Also, I know, from yet another story, that the human race is in a major time transition on planet Earth. We are moving from the Piscean age to the Aquarian age. For those who don't know or understand how this will impact the human race and the planet, I've included my experience with astrology and the remembering that has been triggered within me to help educate people on what is happening and how to utilize it to their best advantage. This transition is facilitating a mass awakening of souls on the planet. In fact, everything I'm about to share with you is intended to help in aiding this mass awakening so people can see and know themselves as all powerful spiritual beings and how they personally fit into the esoteric world around them and not just the day-to-day struggles of surviving on the Earth plane. It's important to understand that our time here on the planet is designed to heal and evolve ourselves (and the whole human race) so it can move forward into the "Golden Age" on Earth. A time of peace, harmony, fellowship, community and infinite love that has been predicted, if the human race made it into the Aquarian Age.

I share all this at the beginning of the book to explain how I ended up experiencing the life I have had and the importance of sharing it now to facilitate the awakening of souls around the world. A life that filled my tool box with personal stories that I can apply and relate here (hopefully in a humorous way) to help people open up to a different perspective and understanding of their own experiences. I'm hoping my stories will be easily relatable to people who have gone down a similar path to let them know that they are right on target, and easily understandable to the awakening souls that are new on the scene. Also, it is my wish that my messy life will be an inspiration to people not yet living their lives fully, to get out of their boxes and take some chances. Even if it makes them, or the people around them, uncomfortable. If what I share in these pages motivates just one person to make their dreams come true, or makes one person's personal awakening easier, my efforts will not have been in vain. To quote a song from the movie *Rocky Horror Picture Show*, "Don't dream it. Be it." I see now, in retrospect, that my life has been more than my own personal learning, growing, and evolving by my experiences. It also provided me the stories I share here to help others learn, grow, and evolve in their own lives. Everybody is on the path in one way or another. No one is alone on their journey. We are all in this together! This is one of the most auspicious times to be alive in human history as we venture into an evolutionary leap of consciousness the likes of which mankind has never seen before. Together, lets escape the madness of the old paradigm and embark on a journey to awakening in order to create the New Earth of love, compassion and community.

HERE TO SERVE!

Old Souls

Have you ever discovered you already knew something before it happened? Have you ever felt like you have been there before? Are déjà vu experiences frequently occurring? Have you ever felt like you don't belong here because you are different? If you answer "yes" to any of these, you are probably an old soul.

I define a soul in a spiritual sense, not religious. A soul is a spark, or fractal, of the divine energy that has separated from source in order to have a unique experience to enable the Divine to experience itself. A fractal can be thought of as a never-ending geometric pattern repeating itself exactly over and over again that is identical to the original source. Once it is created, it can never be destroyed. This is one of the great mysteries. The soul has no beginning and no end. It is infinite. Some souls have been in creation much longer than other souls.

This is my story. Keep in mind that I didn't know at the time who or what I was, but when I looked back, I could only shake my head in knowing: Ah, I was an old soul. I showed up on the planet in physical form in the late 50's - 1959 to be exact. The last of the baby boomers; the wave that changed the world. My parents were typical of the greatest generation. My father was a carpenter who brought home money, but little else. My mother held up her end of the martial contract and raised the children and took care of the home. Neither were happy. We were picture perfect on the outside, but privately, as dysfunctional as they come. The place was Cleveland, Ohio. "The Best Location in the Nation," was a nickname commonly used for Cleveland in the 1950s, some may argue that has changed in succeeding decades, but I remember it as a great place to grow up.

Reflecting back to my childhood, my first memory at the age of four is that of not wanting to be here. I had a visceral understanding that I didn't fit in. I felt like an alien. Somehow, I knew the family I was born into and lived with was not my own. There was no connection or bond with my parents. I knew I was loved by them but neither of them was loving or affectionate in any way. My two brothers lived much different lives as they were born at much different periods in my parent's marriage. They were the eldest and the youngest. They were totally indifferent to me. It was as if we simply shared a house to live in. It was only my sister that I felt a connection with. We were born two years apart and have the same astrological sign. We just "got" each other. But she was a girl, older, and had a life of her own. Most of the time I felt the need to escape. I spent a lot of my time fantasizing about taking a bottle of aspirin so I could get out of the unloving and chaotic family environment that I found myself in. That fantasy turned into a reality when I was four and I had to get my stomach pumped. I find it amazing when I look back that a toddler would feel this way and act on those feelings. Where did those feelings come from? How did I even know about things like that?

I was brought up by a very Catholic mother therefore I attended a Catholic elementary school. My first day of school in kindergarten was worthy of a picture taking moment to commemorate this rite of passage dressed in my new school uniform. My teacher was a nun dressed in the traditional black robes with the white wimple. There was not even a trace of fun-loving energy emanating from this scary visage. Her energy was more menacing than anything else. On the afternoon of my first day, the Nun gave us each a picture to color in. I think mine was a picture of a fish. For the first time that I can remember, my perfectionism kicked in. I didn't like what I had colored so I rolled it up in a tube and raised my hand to get another picture to try again. The nun came over, saw what I had done and became infuriated. Without a word, she yanked me out of my chair and before I could process what was happening, I found myself bewildered, standing in the garbage can facing the corner wearing my new pressed slacks, crisp starched white shirt, and clip on tie. I spent the rest of the afternoon facing the corner to ponder this brutal, punishing Christian institution that I was going to have to endure. I felt hopeless. Even to my young mind the reality of what I was experiencing was a total contradiction to the rhetoric I was forced to sit through during mass on Sunday mornings. Needless to say, my initial experience on my first day of school set the tone for the next eight years for me.

The major purpose of Catholic school is to indoctrinate young minds with Catholicism, or at least attempt to. I read a quote once from a priest that said, "Give me your child until age seven, and I will give you back a convert for life." He knew how impressionable young minds were and readily took advantage of it. When I studied how people were indoctrinated into cults at a later age, I realized the process was identical to what the Catholic church inflicted on me. Cults use fear, in my case it was burning in hell for all eternity, to control the mind and instill prejudice, hatred, violence, mistrust, lack and scarcity. They keep their converts confused and disoriented with constant contradictions. The greatest contradiction is with their God. First, they teach that he is all loving and forgives anything, then you find out he is angry and vengeful punishing anybody who disobeys him with unimaginable suffering for all eternity. The Nun I had for kindergarten typified this behavior. She presented herself as this loving soul who sacrificed herself to serve God, but in reality, she was an angry, unhappy soul how brutalized little children.

During kindergarten, I was taught that God is all powerful and sees everything. Even if you hid in the closet to eat your stolen cookie, God would know and punish you. No one could hide from God. I was five at the time. When I was seven and in second grade, Catholic children were prepared to make their First Holy Communion. First Holy Communion is a Catholic ritual signifying a child is old enough to receive the Body of Christ (Holy Communion) by eating a wafer which represents his physical body. Upon reflection, the ritual seems rather macabre - eating the flesh of a dead man. However, before you could receive the Body of Christ, you had to purge and cleanse your soul of sin by going to confession and telling a priest about the cookie you ate while you hid in the closet. We had to wait in line to enter a little wooden house on the side aisle of the cathedral. While waiting, I could hear everything that was being said on the inside. The priest, who sat in the center room behind a screen window, would listen reverently while he listed all your transgressions. He then assessed your sins by degrees so he would know what kind of penance to hand out so that you would sufficiently be absolved of the devilish infraction(s). The penance typically consisted of a few "Hail Mary's" and an "Our Father." This religion was all about punishing.

It was plainly apparent to me that the ritual of confession was a major contradiction to what I was taught two years prior in kindergarten. Which one was it? God sees all because it's impossible to hide from him or that God is somehow too busy and needs some underling to run intermediary for him. It was then that I realized that the church, the religion, was just making it up as it went along. How does a seven-year-old have that kind of insight and recognition to see and understand the dichotomy of those two events? My only conclusion is that on some level I already knew that religion was fabricated by man and not to be taken seriously. The experience of confession simply reminded me of that fact. The only way I could have possibly known this, was that I brought the knowledge with me when I incarnated into *this* life. A knowing like that is much more than intuition. It must be pre-programmed information. There was no question on my part. It was an absolute fact to me at the time. Pretty impressive for a seven-year-old. My days of being a Catholic ended in the confessional.

In my late teens and early twenties, I explored different theologies but nothing seemed right. There seemed to be something missing or a contradiction that didn't feel right to me. I made several attempts to read the bible, but never made it very far. Finally, I just accepted it wasn't a book I was supposed to read

---

✿

I was bullied through most of my elementary school years. I was obviously different. I was quiet, sensitive, and not very competitive, like most boys of that era were expected to be. If somebody wanted to prove their awakening masculinity, they looked around for an easy mark to prove themselves by dominating or torturing them. There I was, the easiest of all marks. I never fought back, either verbally or physically, so bullying me was a sure thing. I however did become a fast runner with my long spindly legs. They had to catch me first!

The bell would ring at the end of the school day and I would run out of the building like a bat out of hell. It was my way of making sure I was far ahead of the pack so nobody would bother me. It was a mile walk to get home from school. After a few blocks I would relax and enjoy the scenery. One day, I was almost home when this mean redhead that I knew from school went after me. I can still see his face to this day. He was a sixth grader, a couple of years ahead of me, and always in trouble. I thought he looked older than a typical sixth grader, so I assumed he flunked once or twice. He was walking on the other side of the busy street from me. I don't know what caught his attention, but he ran across the street causing horns to blow and pushed me to the ground. With his black pointed leather shoe, he kicked me in the head. I remember my face going numb. From out of nowhere, a high school kid appeared and pulled him off me and the redhead ran back to the other side of the street. The guy from high school helped get me up from the ground. He steadied me with a hand on each shoulder, looked me in the face, and said "Do you want me to get him for you?" I calmly said, "no." The guy couldn't believe it and asked if I was sure. I nodded my head, I was sure. I don't know exactly what I was thinking, but somehow, I knew that having somebody beat up to avenge me wouldn't help the situation.

I walked the rest of the way home wondering why the world had to be the way it was and pondering why the redhead acted the way he did. It was not the behavior of someone very evolved. He was violent and uncaring of other people and how they may feel. Not an old soul. He had a lot of learning to do. But me, I had the ultimate champion ready and offering to render my revenge and somehow, I intuitively knew that that was not the answer. In that moment I exhibited compassion, empathy, and understanding. Attributes that I know I must have brought into this incarnation from a prior life because I sure didn't learn them at home or at school.

After a lifetime of remembering, I understand that we live in an energetic world with a constant dynamic interplay between the light and the dark energies. I can venture an educated guess as to why the incident with the redhead, and other bullying, happened to me. Light, loving energy makes dark energy uncomfortable. It senses the higher vibration and it tends to lash out at it.

Back to my childhood, other kids my age did not interest me very much. The activities that occupied their time (school, sports, television, hanging out in cliques) held no fascination for me. I was definitely a loner. I spent most of my time riding my bike exploring new territory expanding the world I lived in. I discovered parks where I could play, a river I could swim in, and woods for hiking. I loved being in nature. Surrounded by its beauty, the outdoors provided me with a sense of peace and belonging. I could feel all its good vibrations caressing my soul and inspiring me to dance. I loved to dance in the summer sun, in a swirl of falling leaves, amongst the falling flakes of snow, and the nourishing rains that sustained all life. In nature, my mind opened up and all the wisdom of the ages flowed freely back to me reminding me of who I really was. It was like reconnecting with an old friend that had never really left. Nature was *my* church. It's where I went to feel close to the Divine.

As an adolescent, one of my favorite things to do was look up into the sky and wonder what was beyond it. I was also looking for spaceships. It was the sixties and alien abductions were on the cover of all the supermarket tabloids. I don't know why I thought the aliens only came at night, but I would gaze up at the stars and implore the aliens to come and take me away. I saw it as a win-win situation. I would get off the planet and away from the primitive, violent people, and those I had nothing in common with. I figured the aliens had to be more advanced than the ones here on Earth, so I would be going to a better place. I already felt like an alien myself in the world I was growing up in. Maybe I thought they would take me home to the place I was originally from. I don't remember exactly. I just knew I didn't want to be here. Fortunately, it never happened. I had much to do here in this lifetime. What I think is striking now is that I was never afraid. I was eager to embrace new, different, and exciting experiences.

My life changed when I discovered that I lived a few miles from the beach. I can recall the exact time it happened. I was about ten years old, riding my bike through the neighborhoods when I turned a corner and much to my surprise, there was Lake Erie! After that I was officially a beach bum. I loved being in the water and playing in the surf even though the water was usually pretty cold. If I couldn't escape the world by being abducted by aliens, I could easily escape it by being under water. I learned to hold my breath for long stretches of time so I could float below the surface. Escaping gravity for a while was magical to me. It was quiet and peaceful, void of all distractions. It was like my internal consciousness became my entire focus. Also, I could do nifty things with my body that I could not do on land. It truly was like being in another world. It would be much later in life I would find out why I always gravitated to water.

During the fourth grade, I discovered equestrian literature and became an avid reader. After I devoured every horse book in the library, I graduated to cheap dime store novels that were filled with adult drama and sex. A world I wanted to be a part of. Reading was another form of escape for me. Nothing better than getting lost in a good book. I learned a lot about the world and its various exotic places and the people that inhabited them. Reading opened me up to the struggles that other people had to endure and how those struggles facilitated growth and understanding. It helped me understand human nature. I liked diversity and learned to appreciate it. It expanded my view of the world and its varying perspectives. I learned to weigh and evaluate life and draw my own conclusions. I believe people who try to ban books don't want others to develop the ability to expand, think, and grow because it makes them more difficult to control.

In ninth grade, there was a short period I went through when I began spending time with a group of kids that were each different in their own ways. They called themselves the O'Blocks. They used the first letter of each of their last names to come up with the title. I felt honored that they changed it to the O'Blorcks to accommodate my last initial. It was fun to have friends to hang out with but it didn't take me long to notice I did not have much in common with them. Sadly, my membership didn't last long. I was already leading an adult life that I didn't feel I could share with them. My short tenure made it obvious that I was far more mature than most people my age. I was done with being a kid.

After that, my life changed quickly. Most of my friends were college aged or older. I even had friends in their thirties. I seemed to fit right in even though I was only fourteen. It was easy and natural. It helped that I happened to look older as I was always tall; six feet tall by the age of twelve and growing. I was articulate, well read, and handled myself with a maturity some adults had not yet attained. I was attentive and inquisitive, with an insatiable curiosity about people. I mastered being quiet and listening early in life. I listened to the universe, to the planet, and most importantly, to my intuition. It was always there working for me, guiding me through the gauntlet of my friends' adulthood experiences. I naturally had a sixth sense about people and situations that I learned to trust. It was visceral. I could feel people's energy and the energy of a situation. Things would be going great, everybody having a good time, then somebody would say something inappropriate that people took offense to and I would literally feel the room go cold with the palpable discomfort. Luckily, I didn't take things very seriously; except in debates about whatever issue was current at the time. I laughed easily, and was easy going. My company was sought after. I was wise beyond my years. And of course, I wanted to have fun! I suppose it also didn't hurt that I had a look that was in vogue in the 1970s - think young Robert Redford.

Albeit, my life wasn't all fun and games. I began spending much more time alone deep in thought letting my consciousness roam freely. My favorite place to think was at the beach. It was a small crescent of sand just west of downtown Cleveland that was only a half mile long. Even in winter, I would walk back and forth thinking about things. I tackled some big theories and philosophies for somebody still in their teens. I remember after seeing *The Incredible Shrinking Woman* with Lily Tomlin, I had the nature of the universe all figured out. The main character gets smaller and smaller. As she shrinks, the space around her gets bigger and bigger revealing more. This was my first exposure to a quantum world, even though I didn't know it at the time. In this version of the story, the movie ends with the main character starting to grow larger, leaving the viewer to wonder how big would she get? I envisioned her outgrowing the planet and then the galaxy and eventually incorporating the whole universe. Suddenly, I had a realization that this could be used to describe the universe as the body of God. I had taken an anatomy class my first semester in college. I now understood the structure of the body being made up of cells which had a whole world inside each of those cells. I theorized that planet Earth was just one of trillions of cells inside the body of God floating around like a blood cell does. The movie *The Fantastic Four* comes to mind when they shrink a spaceship to travel inside the human body to destroy a disease that was afflicting it. I went as far as to think that the human race was a parasite negatively afflicting the planet Earth. Given my knowledge and understanding at the time, I believed it was a good metaphor for God. I'm still amazed that I came up with this idea without any education or training in the realm of metaphysics and spirituality. This story is typical of the knowledge that I inherently possessed and the advanced thinking that it facilitated. I began to recognize myself as a co-creator with the Universe or God. I realized that I was an old soul that trusted my intuition to expand my consciousness of the nature of the Universe, which I could utilize to manifest on a daily level.

Trust me, I'm not an egotist trying to inflate myself above and beyond everybody else. I don't feel like I was anything extraordinary. I share my early maturity and advanced understanding to demonstrate that some people/souls come into their lives with a knowing that was gleaned from previous lives. I easily saw through the church's dogma because on some level I already had the experience and knew it wasn't right for me. I was naturally compassionate, empathetic and understanding because I had mastered those attributes in a previous life. I didn't waste a lot of time being a child because I already possessed an adult-like maturity and didn't have to relearn that this time around. These are all attributes of old souls and how they manifest easily and early. I always had a prevailing sense of "been there, done that." A *knowing* without an explanation of how I knew. Old souls are more common than what you might expect and are coming in at a faster rate than ever before to help facilitate the transition. If only to be a point of love and light to keep the energies balanced as the darkness is exposed.

I now understand that we are the sum total of all our past experiences in this life and all our lives. Look at your own life from birth to this moment. Can you look back and see how everything you experienced and everything you learned from those experiences made you into the person you are today. Now factor in the idea that we are eternal beings living lifetime after lifetime. Take a moment to try and expand your understanding to encompass all the lives you have lived previously and the ones you will live after this one to see that we are evolving *beings*. We are not living a singular experience. We carry what we learn in one life into the next and then the one after that and the one after that...into infinity! We spend our time here on Earth having experiences that trigger memories of prior lessons. Once we learn/remember a lesson, it's over and done with. We don't have to keep doing the same thing over and over again. Knowledge keeps accumulating. Through this process we, and the human race evolve.

After enough time, maybe eons, transformation of an entire planet occurs. I believe that's what is happening on the planet now. We are in the middle of a planetary transformation! The souls that are incarnating now are more than just old souls. They are more advanced than ever. An army of beings coming into the Earth plane to finish the job! My generation laid the groundwork and established a foundation for them to build on. I was born at the perfect time to witness, facilitate, and help complete the transition. One of the ways I'm doing that is to share my innate understanding such as astrology, and life experiences in this book. Pretty amazing! Makes me wonder what our potential really is.

E XPERIENCE LIFE!

Planetary Toolbox

Astrology has been around ever since man started recording history. The Egyptians elevated it to a revered science as a tool to explain the world. The scribes, usually in a priestly role, were consulted about everything. Even the placement of their monumental buildings was determined by the movement of the stars. Pharaohs and priests depended on astrologers to guide them in decisions that affected the people they ruled. Hindus use astrology to determine suitability of couples in the arranged marriage process. It is also used to find the most auspicious date and time for the wedding to take place. In fact, world leaders all through the ages have used astrology to help them navigate to their end goal. Even our modern-day United States Presidents have had astrologers on their payrolls. As the industrial age rushed us into modern times and lights brightened the night skies, the average man has lost touch with their connection to the stars and their credibility. Astrology has become a cultural entertainment on the comic page of newspapers. This is changing as more people are reawakening to the power of the moving planets and learning their intricacies to understand the circumstances of their everyday lives.

It would be difficult to talk about my life without providing a little bit of background information on astrology since I will often reference it. People tend to assume that I am an astrologer. I tell people it is simply a hobby of mine. I don't refer to it on a daily basis. I don't think it controls us or predicts what is going to happen. Certain placements and aspects have different energies that can be utilized. I think it is helpful to know what kind of energies we are working with at any given moment so we can make the best possible decision to manifest a desired outcome out of a world of infinite possibility. The future truly is being manifested moment by moment by our thoughts and the thoughts of the world at large; personal versus global. Astrology is an exact science that gets surprisingly complicated. It helps if you have excellent memory and good math skills if you want to pursue it. It is so much more than just your sun sign. The sun signs are the twelve signs of the zodiac that you can be born under given your date of birth. It is layers upon layers of placements, aspects, progressions, transits and things I don't even know about that all take math to figure out all happening in a third dimensional universe. There is so much to remember that goes way beyond my understanding. I have never been noted for having a good memory. All of this forces me to stick to my original description that, for me, it is just a hobby. A hobby that I use for everything I contradictorily say.

Other people might argue the contrary. In the late 1990s, I went on a wagon train adventure with my sister and her family in Wyoming. I became friends with one of the tour guides as we would spend entire days horseback riding through the wilderness of Grand Teton National Park. Her name was Aubrey. We enjoyed comparing our very different lives. She was a Mormon from Salt Lake City working her way through university and I was a massage therapist from a big city back east. I learned a lot from her. One morning, when she was on breakfast duty, she came over to our table and started chatting. I forget what the conversation was about, but whatever it was she said made me curious as to what sign she was astrologically, so I asked her. She smiled and congenially asked me if I was "into astrology?" I quickly replied, "No, it's just a hobby." My pre hormonal nephew James who was quiet until now burst out, "Hobby?! Hobby my foot. He won't get out of bed if Mercury is

Retrograde!" Everybody laughed and the conversation continued. Later, when we were on our daily ride into the wild, I had to laugh to myself that my sister's kids knew me as well as they did. He was right though, beware the Mercury Retrograde. It was good to know the kids were paying attention. I wondered what else they were picking up from their unusual uncle?

Here are a few of the experiences I have had with Astrology throughout my life.

It was always fun to read about my sun sign when I was young because the descriptions of people with my sign seem accurate. It was like they were describing me, but I never took it seriously. I wasn't motivated to get a real astrological reading until I was twenty-six years old after a long relationship ended and my life circumstances changed drastically. Even then it was only for the fun of it. Somebody I knew had previously used a particular astrologer and they said her reading was amazingly accurate and I thought why not. It was the first and last time an astrologer gave me a whole life reading in an hour-long session. I still have the chart she made for me.

Usually, an astrologer will only tell you what the energies are for an upcoming year. I guess it's good for business if they have you continually coming back. This first one, sorry I don't remember her name, told me three things that over the years, turned out to be spot on. First, she said I wouldn't have any children of my own but that there would be two children that I would be very close to. This played out exactly. I ended up being a father figure to my sister's two children. To this day we are all good friends and enjoy sharing life's ups and downs together. I'm always there for them if they need me.

Second, the astrologer said that my 32nd year would be the best year of my life. I thought that was kind of inappropriate at the time. What about the following seventy years? Now that I'm in my sixties and I can look back on my life, I have to admit that, so far, she was right. It was the best year of my life. When I was thirty-two, my career finally took off and I was able to afford a great apartment that became the social center for my group of friends. I was a success! I had money flowing in, great friends, and several hot romances. I had a lot of fun that year. The third prediction was that my fifties would be the most difficult time of my life. Unfortunately, that couldn't have been more accurate. That's a story I have saved for a later chapter.

During my thirties I worked with the nationally renowned astrologer Buz Myers. He was the astrologer to then President Bill Clinton. His hometown was where I lived and he came back and took appointments a few times a year. A friend of somebody I was dating, connected me with him and I'm so thankful she did. His work was always focused on spiritual growth and evolution. By then, I was well along in my spiritual awakening so that was perfect. He always provided great tools to advance my learning and understanding. He was expensive so I only worked with him every other year. He was my biannual birthday present to myself. He either kept fantastic notes or had an amazing memory because at every visit I felt as though I had just recently seen him. My sessions with him were always jaw dropping. It was noted by him once that all my relationships lasted about two weeks, which was true. Then he added I was happy to see them go. I just sat there and laughed because that couldn't have been truer. Buz took astrology to all new levels for me. I learned a lot about the modality, the nature of the universe, about myself and my place in the universe, and the path that I was on. He pointed out that my entire life was about healing; being healed so I could heal others.

Buz rented a hall in 2000 and gave predictions for the new millennia. All of his predictions have come to pass. He predicted that the internet and communication would explode and that it would become impossible to keep secrets and that corporations, especially tech industries, would become huge and control governments and set the norms for society. He also saw trouble ahead for the housing market and banking. Remember 2008? You can be the judge of that.

I heard through the grapevine that Buz was fighting some medical issue that proved to be fatal. Even though he never talked about it, he must have known he was going to pass soon. At our last session, when it ended, he came around from his desk, put his arm around my shoulder and walked me to the door. He had never done that before. He paused as he opened the door, turned to me with a conspiring gleam in his eye, and told me that the relationship I dreamt about was out there. He told me to be patient because they weren't ready for me yet. Many, many years later he turned out to be absolutely right.

A year later, I went to a dinner party at my best friend Kris's house. One of her guests was a young woman named Emily. Kris intentionally invited her so that we could meet. She was an astrological savant. She was only twenty years old so her ability had to be from many past lives. When dinner was over, Emily asked for a volunteer to have their chart read in front of everybody as our entertainment for the evening. My hand went up instantly. She pulled up my natal chart on her preferred astrology site and examined it. Then she gave me her interpretation of it. Everything she said was spot on. The big takeaway from the reading was that I would be touched by love two more times in life, once when I was 48 then when I was 58. A questioning look crossed her face when she gave me the prediction. She paused quizzically then added that she wasn't sure if it would be with the same person or not. I was forty at the time. As it turned out, she was absolutely correct.

It was hard to replace Buz so a long time went by before I enlisted the help of an astrologer again. I had gone back to school in my forties to get a teaching degree. I was getting ready to graduate and make a big career change. I wanted to confirm that I was moving in the right direction, so it was time to take a leap of faith and trust somebody new. Every year for my birthday I got an invite, and discount, to try the astrologer that had taken over for Buz. I figured if Buz thought they were good, then they must be. I decided to give her a try. Her name was Joanne. She lived in Virginia, so we worked remotely.

When I work with somebody new, I don't give them any background information or direction in the reading. I figure the astrologer should know everything by looking at my chart. Joanne spent the whole session talking about all the relationships I was going to have in the following year. That my life was going to be like a Hollywood movie with hot romance and exotic travel. She finished by telling me that I was going to move in a year. She never once brought up school, career, or work. I let her talk the entire time while I thought to myself that she couldn't be further from my reality. I hadn't dated anybody in years and the last thing on my mind was moving after I just spent the last five years restoring a beautiful old house that was my dream come true. When she was all done, I told her I had enlisted her services because I was finishing school and thinking about making a career change. She got quiet. I could literally hear her checking my chart over the phone. All she said was the energy that saw me as moving could in fact be a career change. That was that. The session ended and I sat there and thought what a waste of money the last hour was.

Well, if she wasn't right about everything! Four months later I met somebody that rocked my world. He traveled for a living and flew me all over the country so we could spend time together and get to know one another better. The astrologer said I was going to have a lot of relationships, but it turned out to be just the one. What she must have been seeing was that since it was a long-distance relationship, we were only going to get together once a month. The courtship was off the charts. Joanne was right! It played out just like a romantic Hollywood movie. After a year, I couldn't take the long distance anymore and sat my new love down for a heart-to-heart. I told him one of us had to move so we could be together all the time or we needed to end the relationship. He was adamant that we needed to be together. Unfortunately, since I was the one starting a new career, it turned out to be me. I couldn't believe it. Joanne wasn't right about everything!

The next story I'm going to share isn't about what I was told was going to happen, it is a story that explained *why* something happened. I did end up in a relationship with "Mr. Hollywood" which lasted eight years. It ended badly, as relationships sometimes do. I was left without a home, no job, and no available funds. I didn't know what to do or where to go. I just knew I couldn't share a house with this man while we waited for it to sell. I ended up moving to Fiji. That lasted a couple of months before I decided that wasn't the best decision I could have made. Ultimately, at age 52, I ended up living with my mother until the house sold and I got some money to start over again. I couldn't have been in a worse situation. A close friend of mine took the liberty of looking up my astrology to see what was going on. I was shocked when I was informed that I had not one, but three Pluto transits going on that would be affecting me for the next two years. The first one hit my chart on the exact day the relationship started to implode.

For reference, Pluto is the planet of death, transformation, destruction, renewal, and rebirth. It empowers us to confront our deepest fears and recognize any self-destructive habits, patterns, or beliefs that keep us stuck repeating the same experience over and over again. Usually, a person will get at least one Pluto aspect in the course of their lives. After all, we are all here to learn and grow. I was getting hit with three simultaneously! To quote my friend, "That is unheard of!" Knowing this made the experience more palatable. Instead of feeling like a victim, I was able to see it as a positive. What needed to be healed, what did I want to let go of, what did I want to create? I love reading about the Pluto aspects. They always end with, "When it is over, your life will be totally different than when it began." That couldn't have been truer in my situation! Three years later, I found myself living in paradise embracing my spiritual family that I had always longed for.

Years later, I met the man that I'm sure Buz was referring to. We decided to get married. I used astrology as a tool to imbue the marriage with the best energies possible to assure its success. I always said if I ever got married, the wedding would be in October when the sun sign Libra rules. Libra, an air sign, is all about peace, love, harmony, and balance. Each sign represents something in the human experience and Libra is the sign of relationships. That easily narrowed it down to a thirty-day window. Next, I had to look at where the moon was during the month. The moon stays in a sign for two to three days. There can be a space of time before the moon moves into the next sign called "moon void of course." This may last minutes or hours. It's not recommended that decisions be made or contracts signed during this time. I looked at weekend dates and saw that the Moon was in Leo on Saturday, October 2nd. Leo, a fire sign, made the perfect choice for the emotional aspect of the marriage because it is about love, romance, play, loyalty, and protectiveness. The hardest part was settling on the Rising sign. This is more challenging because the Rising sign changes every two hours making a particular sign available only once a day. With our sleep schedule, night and morning hours were not an option. That narrowed it down to five choices. Lucky for us, Taurus was a possibility between 7:30 pm to 9:30 pm. Taurus, an Earth sign, is about beauty, sensuality, dedication, stability, reliability, and longevity. Between these three planetary energies, we felt that we gave our marriage the perfect tools for a fun, loving, and successful marriage that would stand the test of time. When I told our family and friends how we came upon the day and time for the ceremony, they shook their heads knowingly and laughed.

For anybody who may be interested, a Mercury Retrograde is when the planet appears to move backwards in the sky. It happens three times a year for about 20 days. Mercury rules communication, transportation, and technology. It is not wise to sign contracts or make big purchases because you may end up having to do it twice. Be prepared for traffic and travel mishaps and delays. Technology breaks down and misunderstandings abound. It has become a cultural joke. When something goes wrong, invariably you will hear somebody ask if Mercury is retro. I was born under a Mercury Retrograde so I tend to navigate them with ease - lucky me!

My hope is that sharing these stories of how my life was gifted by astrology will open your mind to its possibilities. You can easily see why I use it as reference points to help understand and give meaning and purpose to my life, why I attract the people I do, and how to best navigate events so I can make the most of whatever comes my way. Almost all of my stories in the remainder of this book have an astrological addendum to help understand how and why things happened the way they did.

I use astrology to find out what is in a person's personal tool box. What are they working with that they were gifted at the moment of their birth? I can use it to see what kind of energies are going on in one's chart at any given time. The latter could explain why something is happening and how to best approach it. We are always in the driver seat. Places and events also have an astrology based on the moment they were created. For instance, when a city is founded, the date, time, and location it occurs determines the energy that space will hold. I can also see how astrological energies are affecting the world on a global basis.

Let me qualify that by giving you a brief explanation as to how all this works. Remember, I'm not an astrologer, I just find it fascinating.

At the moment of birth, of anything not just people, the planets in our solar system are frozen in time and their exact positions are plotted on a pie diagram consisting of twelve slices, or houses, called a natal chart. The whole pie diagram contains 360 degrees just like any circle and each house has 30 degrees in it. Each house rules a different aspect of the human experience: home, career, relationships, family, etc. Planets are plotted by what degree in the circle of the natal chart they are. How they figure that out is still a mystery to me. The exact time of birth determines whatever sign is at the beginning of your first house and becomes your Rising Sign. I haven't figured that out either. I just look at charts in the book or use a computer program to glean the information I need. All the other signs progress around the chart counter clockwise giving you the kind of energy that will influence that particular house and the planets in it. The planets, when plotted on the chart affect the house they fall in and form relationships to each other. The relationships are called aspects. There are six major aspects: conjunctions, sextiles, squares, trines and oppositions combining with 11 major celestial bodies. I estimate that there are roughly 500 aspects. The moon will fall into a particular house depending on its transit in degrees at the moment of birth. Whatever the sign of the particular house will be the sign of the moon. This is a rudimentary explanation. Already over your head? I know the feeling. That's why I say it's just a hobby of mine.

Diagram 1

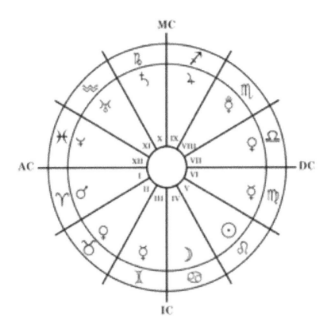

In the above Natal Chart, it shows the AC which is the ascendant, or rising sign, to the left. It also marks the first house. The symbols in each house represent the sign and planet that are the natural rulers of that house.

Before you are totally turned off, let me simplify. There are, on average, about twenty-five major aspects in a person, place, or things chart. The combination of these makes the individual the unique person they are. We are a blend of the aspects. Some are more powerful than others and may cancel the weaker one out. Or, an energy may be more influential at a specific time of life, young versus old. I look at the big three; the Sun sign, the Rising sign, and the Moon Sign. With these three you can get a pretty good handle of the person's personality characteristics. This can be helpful when looking at the compatibility between people.

As in life, keep in mind there is always a positive and negative energy to everything in astrology. Either can play out or both. It depends on what else is happening in the chart. Here are brief explanations of the big three:

Sun Sign – This gives a person their basic personality characteristic. For example, Leo gifts the person with a magnetic personality, sunny disposition, playful dynamic, and energetic. But it can also make them insecure, self-centered, and egotistical. These are just a few of the many attributes.

Rising Sign – This is how you present yourself to the world. Basically, you are one way because of your sign but the world sees you given the attributes of your rising sign. For instance, Virgo is organized, clean, practical, and loyal. But they can be judgmental, stubborn, and overthinking. I always refrain from guessing somebody's sun sign even when they insist because I will usually pick up on their rising sign first because it is more outwardly noticeable.

Moon Sign - This is how a person demonstrates their emotion or what governs their emotional life. For instance, if somebody has an Aquarius Moon, they would need a lot of space in a relationship because Aquarius is the sign of the loner. They are also immensely emotional and even the tiniest thing can hurt them, but they will rarely show it because they keep their emotions to themselves. Aquarius moon people are up-beat, compassionate, and easy going but can be detached and aloof, never letting anybody get too close to them. The moon sign is important to think about when considering an intimate relationship with somebody.

If you know the big three signs (Sun, Rising and Moon), you can gauge who and what a person, place, or thing is about and proceed accordingly. You really can't expect a person to be one way if the attributes they carry in the tool box from their signs don't support those qualities.

Before I go any further, for those of you who may be curious as to what's in my toolbox, let me indulge you. I have a Leo sun with Virgo rising and an Aries moon.

A natal chart is frozen at the moment of birth and never changes; however, the planets keep moving. It is said when a planet is moving through somebody's chart, it is transiting. The moving planets at any given time relate to the planets frozen in their natal chart, creating aspects that are going to affect that person at that given moment in time, blessing the person with the energy of that specific aspect or transit. The energy that we are working with is changing constantly. Aspects can be short lived by moving through in minutes or they can last years. Let me describe it another way. Take a natal chart and lie it flat. Plot the current planetary position, or any other moment in time, on a pie chart that you can see through like a piece of velum. Place that chart on top of the natal chart and the new aspects that are created between the two charts can be seen. These new aspects affect you day to day, year to year. This is how you would do your daily astrology if you were so inclined.

Keep in mind that a person, place, thing, or an event has an astrological chart that governs it. The following are examples of each:

A thing can be a business. The exact moment a business is created, usually when the legal papers are signed, and the business becomes its own entity is the key to understanding it. Plot the position of the planets in that moment like you would in a birth chart. This becomes the natal chart for the business. If you have the luxury of picking a day and time, try to find the moment that would give the business the tools needed to be successful. Of course, that may vary given what kind of business it is. You can shop for the perfect natal chart to enhance a business to ensure it has the tools for success.

If you want to find the perfect place on the planet to live, there is a branch of astrology called Astrocartography. It takes a natal chart and superimposes it on the Earth's astrological grid. This tells a person what kind of energies would be prevalent to utilize on any given point on the globe. Simply read the can pursue description for each line closest to the place you'd like to move to see the energies you'd be working with. I've used this to find the best places to move to when I wanted to make a change in my life.

The astrology for an event can be useful when planning something like a party or a conference. Look for the best energies available that would support the success of the experience at hand. You would want a different energy for a business conference versus a wedding.

That concludes my tutorial on Astrology. If your interest is piqued, there are volumes of material through the local library, internet, and lots of free seminars that you can pursue to go more in depth. It is entertaining when you get to learn more and see how it plays out in your personal life. Careful though, you might get hooked like me.

WRITTEN IN THE STARS!

Drug Russ

I was taking a break from the sweaty dance floor one hot summer night in 1984 when I met Russ. I was impatiently standing in line to use the restroom. I turned around to check out what I was missing on the dance floor, but what I saw instead were the eyes of the man standing in line behind me who looked straight into my soul. When our eyes met, he gave me what I would come to know as his infamous lost puppy dog grin. He would use this often on me throughout the years. The look said "Please looove me." I instantly recognized him from the beach that I frequented most afternoons. He was always doing calisthenics in a bright yellow speedo – hard to miss! Lately, he had been doing push-ups on a rusty metal frame that had washed ashore. His physique was a muscular build that would catch anybody's attention, especially mine. He was unusually handsome with a square face, full lips, and a wide nose, which was accented with deep brown eyes that appeared like black holes. His eyes transfixed me. I had read somewhere that the eyes were the window to the soul. This guy looked exceptionally soulful. I smiled and acknowledged that I recognized him from the beach. We began flirting until it was my turn to use the loo. When I was done relieving myself, I started to head back to the dance floor. Instead of taking advantage of being next in line, Russ turned and followed me. He didn't even have to piss. He was clever in setting up the situation for us to finally meet. Apparently, he had been trying hard to get my attention for a while, hence the calisthenics at the beach. He had positioned himself behind me in the restroom line in hopes that I would turn around.

Now that he had my attention, he wasn't going to let the moment pass. He asked me if I wanted to get out of the steamy, crowed bar and go for a ride to let the night air cool us off. I agreed that it was a brilliant idea and off we went.

Russ had an expensive car, a new, tan colored, Buick Park Avenue which was way more comfortable car than my beat-up mini truck. Taking his car instead of mine was a no brainer. He knew just where to go. We parked in a field which overlooked Lake Erie, not far from downtown. He offered to share some pot, which turned out to be pretty powerful. I typically prefer not to smoke because when I do, it empties my head of all thoughts and I can't string two words together to save my life. The moment seemed to call for it so, against my better judgment, I decided to imbibe. We sat in silence as the pot started to take effect and just stared into each other's eyes. In the dim light and my hazy mind, they looked like they were filled with all the wisdom of the universe. I found them hypnotic. Time seemed to stop and the moment stretched out into eternity. I was surprised by how comfortable I felt with my new friend. I was able to let go of the physical world and marinade in total comfort and bliss. An unusual thing for me. I never wanted the moment to end. I don't remember much else from the evening. I don't even think we kissed. Eventually, our dreamy, marijuana state evaporated and he drove me back to my truck.

We must have managed to exchange phone numbers because we ended up seeing each other every day for the next two weeks. He was a real party boy, smoking and drinking every day. On Saturday nights, we did mescaline, which was a speedy, mild hallucinogenic popular in the 1980s. It made everything funny and gave me enough energy to dance till dawn. The second Sunday, Russ woke me up from a late afternoon nap with a decanter of brandy to get us in the mood to go out later. At that moment, I knew I didn't want my entire life to be fueled by alcohol and drugs. Don't get me wrong, that time of my life was all about having fun and partying. I just didn't want to do it every day. I pulled back from the budding romantic relationship with Russ and started thinking that we would be better off as friends. I didn't want to just walk away from him. I liked Russ a lot, and for some unknown reason, I felt unusually comfortable with him. He was somebody I could let my guard down with and be unabashedly myself, rather than the public persona I had created. In addition, he was fun and exciting and I love to be entertained.

Russ was not deterred by this. He had finally managed to get my attention and make his way into my life - he was not going anywhere. Although we didn't see each other every day at this point, he always seemed to be around. I was finishing up an art degree and he was a photographer who was trying to make a name for himself. He would show up at night while I was working on projects for school and would often help by giving welcomed creative advice. He saw us as the two budding artists that were going to take the art world by storm. He was inspiring. On nights when I was driving around bored looking for something to do, I would invariably end up at his house. When we were together, we inevitably ended up having sex. I didn't think of us as dating or having a romantic relationship rather more of friends with benefits. I naively assumed he looked at it the same way.

We were a good match for one another. He was an Aries (a fire sign like mine) which gifted him with a creative ability, ever-flowing energy, and the ability to think out of the box. He always wanted to go out and be seen. While I was easily bored with most people, Russ captivated me. Most people lived life by the rules and Russ instigated one law breaking adventure after another. It was all very exciting!

A few months in, Russ called me on a Sunday and asked me to go out dancing. I loved to dance so he knew I would say yes. On Sundays, the big dance club to be seen at was called Traxx. It was located downtown Cleveland in the old warehouse district that was beginning to see a renaissance. We parked a block away and had to walk down the street to get to the club. On the way, I ran into somebody I briefly dated. I stopped to chat for a bit and see how life was treating him. Russ paused to wait for me but I waved him on and yelled that I would meet him inside.

His name was David. Another artist type with a head of thick, bouncy, auburn curls. He had an unusual funky card shop right downtown in a historic arcade. It carried funny, erotic avant-garde notions that could keep me laughing for a whole afternoon. He must have been successful because he also had a trendy loft studio apartment in the slowly gentrifying warehouse district around the corner from the bar we were standing in front of. I liked him a lot and would have been open to a relationship except for one small problem. I didn't like his scent. He was a vegetarian and I thought his breath smelled like rotten vegetables all the time. Not conducive to kissing, which was problematic as I loved to kiss.

David and I watched as Russ entered the bar. When he reached the door, he turned to me with a big smile and disappeared inside. As soon as he was out of sight, David turned to me and said, "So, you're dating Drug Russ?" I had no idea what he was talking about and asked him what he meant. He proceeded to tell me that Russ supplied the entire gay community with the party drug Mescaline. I was caught off guard and dumbfounded. How do you respond to information like that? I explained to David that we were just friends and that it was none of my business what he did when I was not around. We talked a bit more as we made our way to the dance club. Once inside, we parted ways and that was the last time I saw David.

That night, instead of spending the entire time on the dance floor, I held back in the shadows and observed Russ. As usual, he had people coming up and talking to him all night. What I saw for the first time was money exchanging hands. I was shocked. Damn if David wasn't right. Russ dealt drugs the whole night long! This explained why he seemed to know so many people. Here I thought he was just popular! I never confronted Russ with my discovery. It wasn't any of my business and I would be the last person to judge. After all, I was happy to do the drugs that Russ supplied. I just accepted it. But it gave me one more reason why I would never let the relationship be any more than a friendship.

I do my best to accept people for who and what they are without judgment. "Live and Let Live," is my personal motto. I try to apply that to all aspects of life. Just because something isn't right for me does not mean it is not a good fit for somebody else. I believe morals are a personal objective and should not be legislated, as long as the choices aren't hurting anybody else. Choice is the key here. When somebody is exercising their free choice to have an experience, they should not be denied the opportunity to have it. This is where freewill comes into play. Our will is guiding us to the experiences we need to have to learn and grow. Without these experiences, we wouldn't have an opportunity to do that. We incarnate into the physical realm to have experiences that wouldn't be possible on some other plane or dimension.

Over the next ten years my associations and experiences with Russ became pivotal to my spiritual evolution. The process at times was slow and other times appeared to happen in a flash. I have often mused to myself that we have the ability to rewrite history. A later experience that brings new knowledge and understanding gives an opportunity to go back in time and give an earlier experience all new meaning or perspective. A different way to look at it. I think relating stories to lessons as they were learned makes more sense than sticking to an absolute chronology. I specifically have chosen to weave back and forth between the lessons gleaned from Russ and how I applied them on my own personal journey. I apologize in advance if the telling of my lessons that Russ gifted me with gives the reader whiplash. However, I promise there is a method to my literary madness.

Russ had me reflecting on society and life. Most of the manufactured institutions that govern societies on Earth don't want the masses to learn and grow. They want to keep people ignorant so they can maintain their power and control over us. All of the laws created and all the doctrines written are based on the fear that these institutions will lose their power and control and no longer be able to profit from their positions. Sadly, most people aren't even aware that they are being manipulated and victimized. It all begins the minute a soul is born. Everything a person is taught brainwashes them into believing that the power structure, whichever it may be (a cultural group, a government, or a religion), is benevolent and working for their benefit, but nothing could be further from the truth. Always remember they are all manmade/manufactured and go against the natural order of the Universe.

What makes me the expert in all of this? Nothing! Much of what I know to be true has been inherent in me. As explained earlier when discussing old soul's, I just knew it to be true in every atom of my being. While other things I glean through observation. Going through life with eyes open and choosing to really look and think about something instead of accepting it as pure fact, you begin to see things more clearly. I learned early on to be clear and listen to the Universe. The Universe is always communicating with us. This is a good time to note that I use the Universe as another name for God. As not to confuse the concept with any religion.

I also rely heavily on my intuition. I watch and feel how I react to something viscerally. This guides me to what is true and what is not, as a personal compass. Choosing to trust your intuition more and not talk yourself out of what you're feeling is something that may be beneficial. That small voice or gut feeling is something that should not be ignored, it is often the pathway to your true destiny or path.

This intuition is how I approach books! I have always been an avid reader. Once I was on my spiritual quest, I read every book I could about different philosophies and practices, trying to figure out how life worked. There was a metaphysical bookstore in downtown Cleveland called Manifestations. I became one of their frequent customers. It had that great smell of new books mixed with the scent of a hundred different kinds of incense that transported you as soon as you walked through the door. Some books I read resonated strongly with me and the information they imparted became a part of my belief system. Other books I tried to read didn't feel right and after a few pages I would put them down and move on to something else. I'm always questioning the status quo and asking to be enlightened while leaving myself open to learning. There is always something new to explore, some new topic in a multitude of developing fields, that will move me forward in my understanding. I allow my intuition or intuitive 'knowing' to guide my way to enlightenment and help me remember who I really am and the purpose of my life.

Luckily, I was brought up in a generation that questioned everything. We were taught to think about things, gather evidence, and draw our own conclusions. Yes, I'm talking about the sixties when that first wave of Aquarian energy hit the planet! I'd like to throw in here that astrology played into that. Slow moving planets take years to move through a transit and affect those born into that timeframe. My generation was influenced by Pluto conjunct with Neptune, which says the ideas that were instilled in us by our parents, church, and society would undergo changes until our spiritual and philosophical views are distinctly our own. It is fascinating to look at how the world changed during that time period.

My twenties were a difficult time, as they are for many young adults who are trying to figure out life, the world around them, and how they fit into it. I may have been the happy, carefree, rebel on the outside, but on the inside, I couldn't shake those feelings I had as a child that I didn't belong here. I was depressed with no sense of positive self-esteem and no direction in life. I found myself drifting aimlessly. I was a disaster in relationships, usually hurting the people I was involved with because I didn't know what I wanted. I would fall in love but I didn't know how to be loved. I felt hopeless and that nothing good was ever going to happen.

Valium was a popular anti-anxiety and sedative drug that was easy to get between the 1960s and 1980s. It was easily accessible because it was over-prescribed by doctors. Everybody seemed to have a prescription for it. The Rolling Stones wrote a song about it and called it "Mother's Little Helper." For me, sleep was my ultimate escapism but it didn't come easily because of the lifestyle I was leading. I would use Valium to quiet my demons to quickly fall asleep at night. Nobody knew it at the time, but Valium had long-term side effects like depression, anxiety, and sleep problems. Ironically, exactly what I was taking it for to alleviate.

One Monday night in early spring 1987, my suicidal tendencies got the best of me. My depression hit a new low. My feelings of hopelessness went so deep, it was visceral. I felt like I would never climb out of the hole I found myself. Even with the Valium, I couldn't sleep. I laid in bed allowing my dark fantasies of how I was going to escape the planet get the best of me – and there were many. One of them was jumping off a high-level bridge that spanned the industrial area downtown. Hopped up on Valium, but still unable to sleep at three in the morning, I got in my truck and drove downtown. I knew that this night was going to be the end. I remember yelling and screaming, throwing myself against the car door as I drove, unleashing my pain and suffering building up the energy to throw myself over the rail at the top of the bridge. It was my bottoming out moment; I was crazed.

I drove up the bridge and stopped my truck with one tire up on the sidewalk. I knew exactly where the Cuyahoga River flowed below from countless exploratory walks across the bridge. I got out of the truck and made it to the rail. I was just about to lift my leg over the railing when a car rounded the corner at the bottom of the bridge and headed toward me. I hesitated. I didn't want to scar somebody for the rest of their life by making them witness my demise, so I waited for the car to pass. It never did. It stopped. Before I knew it, Russ was pulling me away from the rail and dragging me into his car. He sat there screaming at me but I didn't hear a word. I sat there comatose, unable to comprehend what had just happened.

The next thing I remember was waking up in bed. I had no idea how I got there or what happened to my truck. I laid there trying to remember what happened, incredulous that I was still on the planet. How could it be? The probability of a car driving up that bridge on a Monday night at three in the morning was unimaginable, in a depressed abandoned downtown area like Cleveland was at the time. The chance that the person driving that car would be somebody I knew seemed even more improbable. And that it would be Russ! It was nothing less than a miracle! I was numb with disbelief. I kept replaying the events over and over in my head trying to make some sense of it. When I was finally able to assimilate and accept the events of the previous night, I realized that there had to be divine intervention because things like that just didn't happen by chance.

This revelation was even more disconcerting because it created so many unanswered questions. Up to this point in my life, I had resisted the idea of a deity that had the ability to intervene, but I was in a place where I couldn't fight it anymore. Nothing like a failed suicide attempt to take the wind out of my sails. In order to move past the moment, I had to surrender to it and open myself up to higher understanding. It was the first time I ever contemplated God as something more than a fictional being passing judgments. This God was an all-powerful benefactor watching out for us rather than the God of religion I was introduced to as a child. Rather, this God was a universal, cosmic, all-loving energy that was guiding us. That morning, as I lay there staring at the ceiling, I had my first conversation with my new understanding of God. I said, and I quote, "Okay God, obviously you want me here. So, if I'm STUCK here, I'm going to be the best that I can possibly be in this life, so I will be that much further ahead in the next." In that moment, my spiritual quest was born. Somehow in doing that, I found peace I had not known before as well as a sense of excitement about the door that I had just opened. What lies on the other side? The next chapter of my life was about to commence.

It is interesting to note here how my mind was suddenly opened to a remembrance that I did not have before. On the day of my suicide attempt, I still held the belief that life was finite and there is nothing, no consciousness, after death. Suddenly, on the day after, without any cognitive thought on my part, I suddenly embraced the knowledge that we are infinite beings living life after life. This is a perfect example of how remembering occurs when you are open and ready to receive new information. I opened up to the idea of God as the Divine and it instantly gifted me information and understanding I did not possess before. My suicide attempt was an evolutionary leap that opened me up to a new, higher level of being.

Russ ended up playing an important role in my life. Because of him, I was still alive. Because of him, I opened up to a higher power greater than me. Because of him, I was able to commence on my journey to discover the spiritual side of my existence. How does one ever honor somebody for something like that?

The following year everything in my life changed. Every book I picked up seemed to hold some deep spiritual meaning. Even the novels I checked out from the library for entertainment. I was moving into places that my friends weren't interested in. Naturally, they fell to the wayside and provided space for people that flowed into my life by what would appear to be randomness, but I thought were actually guided. I was beginning to realize that nothing happened by accident. It all seemed to be a part of some divine plan. Some people call it synchronicity when things mysteriously come together.

One of those miraculous synchronistic experiences led me to taking yoga classes. The instructor became a guru for me, introducing me to a whole energetic world of esoteric understandings, like the chakra system of the energetic vortices of the human body. She would do group sessions on past-life recall that confirmed beyond a shadow of doubt that we are eternal beings that continue to live life after life. Once you have the experience, there is no denying it. I also became addicted to meditation. I started having epiphanies at the strangest times. I remember one Sunday afternoon I was a passenger in a car driving somewhere west. I was watching the farmland roll by when it hit me like a ton of bricks: The best place to be is right where you are. Pretty profound for somebody who always thought that the grass was greener on the other side and was always in a hurry to get there. It seemed such a simple truth. Why hadn't I known it all along?

As I started to evolve, I became more aware and sensitive of the people around me. In trying to discover the origins of my demons and my depression, I realized that everything that happens to a soul from the moment of birth affects that person in one way or another. What I was and how I felt had a direct connection to all of my past experiences. To heal and move past it, I had to acknowledge, understand, forgive, let go, and have gratitude. Not an easy task. There are things I still struggle with all these years later, but I haven't let go of my commitment to get as far ahead in this lifetime as to be that much further ahead in the next. So, for me, giving up is never an option. I realized everybody had a past that contributed to their present. Everybody has a story.

I remembered Russ telling me about how he grew up and how neglectful and mean his parents were. There was a reason why he was angry and why he escaped into drugs and alcohol. On one of our late-night adventures, Russ took me to a rundown, dangerous part of town that many locals were unaware even existed. I sure didn't know about it. It really opened my eyes to how some people had to live. We were passing an entire compound of deserted buildings that were built to house the disadvantaged that had been obviously condemned and were waiting to be torn down. The cheap concrete and masonry construction was still solid. Surprisingly, each unit had its own balcony with three rows of horizontal piping serving as railings. Russ pulled the car to the curb and parked. He turned to me and gave me his sad puppy dog face and said he wanted to show me something. We got out of the car and walked over to the fence. There was a hole in it that he already seemed to know was there. Russ proceeded to squeeze himself through. Without question, I followed. We approached one of the buildings and Russ looked up and appraised the situation. Without a word he started pulling himself up the side of the building using the balconies. Standing on the railing of the first floor he reached up and grabbed the railings on the next floor. I was amazed how easy it was. Yet again, without questioning I followed close behind. My high school gym teacher would have been shocked by my agility. I found myself standing next to him on a third-floor balcony looking into the ruin of an old apartment. Russ still wasn't talking. We walked in through the absent door into a dark, dank, and peeling living space. The negative energy was palpable. I could feel pain and suffering. Russ finally turned to me and looked me in the eyes and said, "This is where I grew up." It was hard for me to comprehend. I couldn't connect my loving gentle friend with the evil energy of the place I was standing in. This time, I was the one who was speechless. In that moment, I realized how blessed I had been to have my own messed up childhood home and family. I took his hand and drew him into my arm and I hugged him tight. I could feel his tears soaking my shoulder as I slowly rocked him back and forth. We stood like that for a long time. Eventually, the moment was over and we made our way back to the car. We sat quietly as he drove. We never talked about that evening. He had successfully managed to convey to me what he wanted me to know but was unable to tell me with words.

Russ had managed to become emancipated at the age of fifteen and had moved out of his family home due to his unsafe living situation, lack of food, his verbally and physically abusive father, and his mother who always stood by her husband and never defended her children. He had befriended two old spinster sisters that had invited him to live with them while he finished high school. I think they may have adopted him but I'm not sure. He took me 'home' to their house a couple of times for Sunday dinner. At the time, the whole situation seemed bizarre to me but I was glad he had some sense of normalcy in his life. It was his attempt at having a real loving family with people who cared about him. I like to think he was including me in his chosen family.

I loved Cape Cod! I would go there every year for a two-week camping trip in August. I always traveled alone. It was more fun that way. If you went with somebody, you ended up spending all your time with that person and never really got a chance to meet any new people, especially the locals who new all the best places to go. When I was by myself, I was much more approachable and it was easier to meet people. I would humorously think to myself that people were taking pity on me, so they would invite me into their social circles. I met many wonderful people over the years that I'm still friends with to this day. Russ didn't really grasp the concept of traveling alone. In fact, I don't recall him telling me that he ever even went on a vacation. In fact, I don't ever remember him going on any kind of vacation ever. The second year I knew him, he tried in vain to invite himself on my camping trip to the Cape, but I ignored his efforts. I wasn't ready to give up the two best weeks of my year.

I was on The Cape for about a week when I returned to the campsite one day and found a note from the manager pinned to my tent. It said to call my mother. I couldn't imagine what it could be about but I knew it couldn't be good. Russ had called my mom and told her that he had been in a bad car accident and asked if she could contact me to let me know that he was in the hospital. I asked her which one. She looked up the number for me and then hung up. I scored some change for the payphone and it wasn't long before I was talking to Russ. He told me he had fallen asleep, or passed out, while driving home on a Saturday night after the bars had closed and the car drove into a brick wall. He injured his left hip badly and required surgery, so he was going to be in the hospital for a while. I tried to be light and airy about it, making jokes so that he would laugh. I could tell in his voice that he was really down and I wanted to cheer him up. I told him about my vacation and how much fun I was having and reminded him that I would be home in another week. I'm sure that didn't help much bit I didn't know what else to say. Instead of cheering him up, he was bringing me down. I got off the phone and started crying. I felt so bad he was all alone in the hospital with nobody to visit or hold his hand.

What I did next still shocks me to this day. I went back to my campsite, broke it down, packed the car and drove home without saying goodbye to anybody. The next day I was sitting beside him in his hospital room, his hand in mine. I had no idea I cared so much about him that I would put my own fun aside to be there for him when he needed somebody to care.

Eventually he healed and life went on. Like everything else, we never talked about what happened. He was left with a slight limp. Watching him walk always made me wonder what really happened. Having to drive by the brick wall that bore the scars of his car frequently didn't help either. Part of me thinks that he was upset I didn't ask him to go with me on vacation. I could imagine him feeling abandoned and disappointed and driving into the wall on purpose. I'll never know. Probably just me and my old habit of taking responsibility for everything. Or, was it some seriously passive aggressive bullshit to get my attention and have me come home. If it was the latter, he succeeded spectacularly.

As I continued to move down my spiritual path of remembering and healing, my energy changed. It became lighter, happier, and definitely more loving to the people in my life and the world around me. As I gained understanding and insight into why I was depressed, it enabled me to become more aligned with forgiveness about circumstances I had no control over. It was becoming difficult for me to be around people who now seemed to be wallowing in negativity, blame, and anger. This included some family members and friends that I had for years. I found myself avoiding them. It wasn't that I stopped loving and caring about them. I just didn't want to be in their company anymore because it invariably brought my energy down, and made me unhappy.

We live in an energetic world. After all, everything, including us, is energy. Low vibrating energy turns into mass to form the physical. Living things have a higher vibrating energy. Disease is low vibrating energy. Homeostasis is higher vibrating energy. Depression is low, euphoria is high. Everything has an energetic field around it which radiates out and mixes with the surrounding energy. That is one of the many reasons why it feels so good to be out in nature. Nature has high vibrational energies, lifting our energies as we pass through it. People's emotional states and intentions radiate energetically too. This can affect someone when they come in contact with it. There is a wonderful book called *The Celestine Prophecy* by James Redfield, that depicts our energetic world perfectly and how we subconsciously are affected by those energies on a moment-by-moment basis.

I definitely didn't want to play the game of our modern society anymore. I was discovering that most people thrive on drama. If somebody else wasn't creating it, they would step in and make their own. I was choosing to create a much different world to live in that was happy and loving. A place where only good things would happen to me. My tag lines became "I'm Happy" and "Be Happy." If somebody asked me how I was, I would instantly respond, "I'm Happy!" When I parted from people rather than saying goodbye, I would say, "Be Happy." In fact, every interaction I had in the course of my day ended with me wishing happiness to whomever.

Putting that kind of energy out has a positive effect in every situation thus creating happiness even if the interaction didn't start that way.

Russ was so entrenched in his anger and suffering he couldn't go to a happy place without chemical assistance. Even that was temporary. There was always the rebound effect. What goes up, must come down. The higher the high the lower the low. It was a roller coaster ride, and I very consciously wanted to get off. We eventually found ourselves living in two different worlds. I didn't spend much time with him anymore. Even though we rarely saw each other, he remained a part of my life. He was always there in the back of my mind.

My road of self-discovery and higher learning kept me busy. I was constantly reading mind expanding books that increased my awareness of the Universe and how it works. I was a magnet for higher vibration people that always had some new perspective or idea to share. As I remembered things, I incorporated them into my everyday life. Yoga and meditation became part of my daily routine, starting and ending my days. Living a healthier lifestyle became a major focus. I went to the gym five days a week in an attempt to build muscle. I changed my diet. I began looking at food as fuel and not something that simply brings pleasure to the taste buds. I spent as much time as I could out in nature, usually by myself. My favorite place was the beach. I purged a lot of negative energy by yelling my anger into the cacophony of the crashing waves on the sand and then recharging by yelling my affirmations into the wind even louder. The woods were another sacred space for me. Walking in the woods so quiet you could hear a pine cone drop, was a close second. If I were a church going person, nature would easily be my church. The forest is a sacred place. That is where I feel most connected to the eternal divine. I still went out dancing a few nights a week. I considered it my aerobic exercise. Moving my body to the music was definitely a high vibration and quite meditative. I decided to stop drinking. My energy was so high from my new practices that alcohol noticeably brought my vibration down. Music and clean living officially became my drugs of choice. I was creating a peaceful, happy place that didn't have the extreme highs and lows I was accustomed to. It was all a good fit for me.

A few years went by before I saw Russ again. It was like he fell off the face of the Earth. I never ran into him when I went out. Nor did anybody ever have any gossip about him. He was the type of guy people liked to gossip about. One day, I went to the lakefront and parked my car intending to walk down to the beach. I never got the chance. Coming up the hill walking towards me was Russ. I was overwhelmed with joy to see him. As the distance between us shortened, I noticed that something was terribly wrong with his face. The lower jaw on one side was gone, his mouth was misshapen and something wasn't quite right about his nose. I can't remember exactly what I felt. I think it was anger because what came out of my mouth was totally inexcusable. Recalling that he ran his car into a brick wall that left him with a limp, I cruelly blurted out, "What did you do to yourself now?" I don't know if he heard me or understood what I said because he didn't respond. He took me into his arms and hugged me. It felt so good; like coming home. We hugged each other for a while, slowly rocking back and forth like we used to do. I pulled away and did my best to wipe the shock off my face. I tried to act as normal as possible.

Instead of walking to the beach, we found a picnic table in the shade to sit and talk. I didn't have much to say. I was all ears to find out what had happened. He explained to me that he had cancer. I don't know how he managed it. He was upbeat about the whole experience. Meanwhile, I was in a state of shock. I couldn't wrap my mind around it enough to ask questions. To this day, I have no idea what kind of cancer it was. All I heard was how the doctors had to cut away this and that to rid his body of it. He explained about all the reconstructive surgery he was going to have and how he was going to be more handsome than ever. He pulled out his now false teeth and showed me what was left of his jaw. He showed me where they were going to take skin to help rebuild his nose. I listened and tried to be as normal as I could without staring. We acted as if discussing these things was an everyday occurrence like telling each other what we had for dinner. He gave no indication of whether he was cured or not and I was afraid to ask.

We sat there all afternoon, sitting in the shade, holding hands. Oddly, it seemed like it was a magical moment for me to be sitting so close to Russ again. When the reality of it started to set in, I became a little angry. I wanted to know why he hadn't contacted me when he found out he was sick. I assured him I would have been there for him holding his hand making sure he was comfortable. I longed to be the perfect friend that stood by and made everything okay. I promised I would start stopping by when I could sit and keep him company. Eventually, one of us had to be somewhere so the afternoon ended. He walked me to my car and we hugged goodbye. Keeping my emotions in check around him had become an ingrained habit. I didn't even tell him that I loved him.

I never saw Russ again.

I made it a habit to stop by his house. He never answered the door. I don't know if he was there or not or if he was just too sick to come to the door. I tried calling, but he never answered his phone and there was no answering machine. I resorted to leaving handwritten messages on his door but there was never a response. Some messages gave specific days and times that I would be coming by, but that didn't work either. When I would stop by again, the messages would be gone. I didn't feel good about any of it.

Three months went by, and I still hadn't heard from him. I was in the bathroom getting ready one morning when the phone rang. It was my mother. She started right away with a warning she had some bad news. Whenever somebody starts off with that you just know somebody passed on. It was Russ. She had just read his obituary in the paper. I held it together long enough to take down the information about a service and hung up. I sank down to the cool tiled floor and uncontrollably sobbed with grief. Russ was only forty-two years old, just six years older than me. How could this be? This was the first time somebody close to me had moved on. My reaction caught me by surprise. It made me feel powerless and empty. There was a place in my heart for Russ that would never be touched by him again. The thought of never seeing him again was unimaginable. I finally understood that grief wasn't sadness about a soul moving on, rather it was something to rejoice about. Instead, grief is a feeling of personal loss for those that are left behind.

I spent the rest of the day reflecting on Russ. I didn't realize how important he was to me. If it wasn't for him, I would have ended my physical life that night when he pulled me off the rail of the bridge. He saved me from myself. His heroic act gave me a second chance at living my life. If it wasn't for him, I wouldn't have had my little chat with God. If it wasn't for him, I wouldn't have opened up to my spirituality. If it wasn't for him, I wouldn't be the man I am today.

Russ passed on in 1995. From my new perspective, I lamented that he wasn't able to forgive his parents and put his horrific childhood behind him and heal himself. His whole life, he took his childhood experience and projected it on to the world around him, recreating an ugly place to live in. Instead of releasing his hurt and anger, he buried it deep down inside himself. Like most damaged people, you would never have guessed at his unhappiness. The persona he showed to the world was all fun and games. I feared he would have to repeat it all in his next life so that he could finally heal it.

When I first found out that Russ had Cancer, I looked it up in my Louise Hay book, *You Can Heal Your Life*. It has become one of my bibles that I often refer to in healing work either for myself, or for friends and clients. Louise Hays noted that certain emotions and experiences had effects on different parts of the body that were consistent with everybody. Another way to put it would be that the physical body represents what's going on at an emotional level. She took it one step further and assigned probable mental causes for physical ailments in the body. For cancer it reads: Deep hurt, longstanding resentment. Deep secrets or grief eating away at the body. Carrying hatreds and feelings of hopelessness. All of these apply in relation to the probable causes for Russ manifesting cancer in his body.

I think it is interesting that the negative energy Russ was holding on to went to the parts of his body that he didn't like and wished were different. Russ was an unusually handsome man. I say unusual because his features were not in vogue at the time. He always complained about his wide face, full lips, and wide nose. I was luckier. Faces featuring blue eyes, blonde hair, thin nose and lips were on the cover of every fashion magazine in the seventies and eighties. Styles change, as they always do, and by the nineties, Russ's features were the epitome of sought after masculinity that every man wanted to have. Unfortunately, not in time for Russ. I found it ironic that the two things about his body that he vehemently didn't like were his nose and his lips and those were the two places where his cancer manifested and had to be cut away. We are creating everything moment-by-moment. Be careful where your mental energy is going because that is what we will create. Don't ever underestimate the power of the mind. Thought, both conscious and unconscious, is the creative force behind everything in the physical world.

Thoughts and emotions are very powerful and need to be expressed and released. It is important not to deny them and allow them to burrow somewhere in your physical body. Pay attention to them! They are clues, or indicators, to what healing needs to take place. Explore and learn healthy ways of expressing and utilizing them to move the negative energy out and allow healing to occur. If we hold onto negative energy and emotions, it will cause disease somewhere in the body. Unfortunately, in many cultures and religions, especially during my upbringing in the United States, people are taught that emotions should not be expressed publicly. This would be a sign of weakness. There are unwritten rules and moral codes as to how people should act that are socially acceptable. These rules need to be abolished and healthy ways to express ourselves need to be taught at an early age. When this happens, there will be a major decline in illnesses, especially cancer, in our society.

I owe many things to Russ. He taught me a lot: to be confident in myself and my artwork, to go beyond what laws may dictate, and to dance to your own tune. Russ ignored the norms and lived his life on his terms, in his way, despite what people said about him behind his back. He may have broken some laws along the way, but in the process, he brought people a lot of happiness. I still have some of his artwork that he gifted me hanging in my home. I also have a black and white portrait of him taken back in his modeling days featured prominently on a wall dedicated to all the people that made a difference in my life. It is my way of not forgetting where I came from and honoring those who helped me along the way.

I don't usually go to memorial services, but I made a point to go to Russ's. I wanted to show the world that people loved him enough to show up and honor him. After it was over, one of Russ's brothers came up to me. I had met him a few times over the years. In fact,

Russ took me as a date to his graduation from university where I was introduced to his sister and his parents. Russ was right, his parents were negative energy amplified. I instantly felt uncomfortable in their presence as they looked condescendingly at me. His brother, on the other hand, was nice and welcoming. He explained to me that he had stayed with Russ in the end and took care of him. I was silently grateful that Russ had somebody at his side caring for him that he knew and loved. His brother asked me to follow him to his car so he could give me some things that Russ requested I have. Out of the trunk he pulled out a medium sized box. Inside was some of his artwork that I had never seen before, his modeling portfolio, some pictures he had taken of me, and believe it or not, a sheet of mescaline. I laughed when I saw the latter. I always appreciated Russ's ironic sense of humor. His drug use was the one thing we fought about and the one thing that prevented me from ever getting in a serious relationship with him. The bequest was duly noted.

I also found a Christmas card in the box. What an odd thing to be left. It looked familiar. I opened it. It was from me! I had signed it with a huge flourish of LOVE, MARK. His brother must have seen the confusion on my face. He stepped up and told me that Russ always kept it at his bedside and opened it often to read. I instantly realized the importance of it. I had made a point to never verbally express my love to him because I never wanted to be misleading. His lifestyle choice made a relationship with him an impossibility for me. Being the stubborn man I can be, I never wavered from that. Sadly, I was well aware of how he felt about me. He never hid his love or his desire to be my partner which made things difficult at times. This Christmas card in my hand was probably the only time I outwardly expressed my love for him. It must have held great value to him if he saved all those years.

I thanked his brother for the box and for being there for Russ when he needed him. I drove home and allowed myself a good cry in the privacy of my apartment. Like Russ, I kept that card on my bedside table for the longest time. For the life of me, after so many moves, I have no idea where it is. I'm sure I will come across it someday.

I spent my thirties and forties acquiring material items and filling up a big house that I had bought at the age of forty. I considered the purchase the opposite of a midlife crisis. I created an art room and modeled it after the one Russ had in his house. Creating art is dirty. You need to have a designated space for it. Then, when I was 45, I met Mr. Hollywood and the following year decided to move across the country to live with him in Arizona. I was going to make the move in a twenty-eight-foot truck which meant I had to purge two-thirds of my belongings which I had spent years accumulating. I wasn't going to have a space for an art room in my new home, so I had to be cutthroat in choosing what I was going to keep and what I was going to get rid of. I was tearing select works I wanted to keep out of one of my sketchbooks when I came across a note from Russ that I had never seen before. In his beautiful handwriting he wrote:

Mark,

> *Just a note of thanks for your thoughts and you being you. I'm hating to say how important it was to have someone go out of their way for me. It was deeply appreciated. Hoping I can be there for you some day.*

Love as always,
Russ XXXOOO

I was dumbfounded! How had I never seen this before? I looked closely at the sketchbook to try and place the time I was using it.

Luckily, I had dated most of the sketches. I was able to infer that Russ must have written the note in response to me cutting my vacation short to be with him after his car accident. He couldn't express his gratitude openly as he wasn't built that way, so he wrote it in my sketchbook for me to find. I couldn't believe it took all these years to come across it. I kept thinking about the timing of it. It was later that same day that I realized his wish was granted. My suicide attempt came after his car accident! He was there for me the night I needed him most.

THANK YOU FOR SAVING MY LIFE!

Mind Body Spirit

I began to call what happened on the bridge that fateful spring night my first miracle. It changed everything in my life because the experience had changed me to my very core. I went from depressed and hopeless to being open and committed to healing and creating happiness in my life. I remembered my words, "If I'm STUCK here, I'm going to be the best that I can possibly be in this life so I will be that much further ahead in the next." I was suddenly open to anything and everything. All it took was a major attitude change, a new perspective, and some direction in order to move me forward in a positive way. New people appeared in my life that blessed me with wisdom and understanding that I had never considered before. The saying, "When the student is ready the teacher will come," proved to be undeniably true. New opportunities and experiences that helped me evolve, spontaneously began to manifest in my day-to-day life. It was all very synchronistic. Books I needed to read seemed to jump off the shelf at me. I would pick them up and caress them. I could feel their good vibrations and got excited about the insight and mastery that lay within. Paying attention and trusting my intuition was the key. I let go of my control and let myself be divinely guided. At times, the quick rate that information was flowing to me and the pace that I assimilated to it all made my head spin. I had never been more excited by anything in my life before this. I loved every new adventure that presented itself.

Yoga suddenly presented itself into my life and captured my attention. To this day, I see yoga as one of the best gifts I have ever received. Let me provide some background here to set the stage for how this happened.

I grew up tall and extremely thin. By the time I was 12 years old, I was already over six feet tall. Being that tall exacerbated my thinness. It's hard to hide when you're that tall and all your classmates haven't reached their growth spurts yet. Unfortunately, in our society, the people that are different and stick out are the ones that end up being teased and bullied. I thought being made fun of for my physicality would end after high school but it continued into adulthood as well. When I was twenty, I was 6'3" tall and weighed 130 pounds with a 28" waist. I was so skinny you could count all my ribs. The teasing was constant. I couldn't take it anymore, so I decided to do something about it!

When I was 21 years old, I took charge of my body and started a fitness regime that quickly turned into a weight lifting fetish. I was desperate to bulk up. Building muscle was going to be my ticket to anonymity. I did this all on my own. I accumulated weights from wherever I could get them and set up a gym in my basement then later in a spare bedroom. I didn't have an experienced friend or a coach to teach or train me. Everything I did, I learned from books. Apparently, that wasn't the smartest thing I could have done because I ended up with really bad lower back pain six years later. I was in such distress that the first thing I thought of when I woke up in the morning was that it was going to hurt to roll out of bed. To me, the pain was worth it. In those six years, I had managed to put thirty pounds on my frame. However, I was still tall and thin, but at least now I was better proportioned, and people stopped making fun of me. Funny how things change. Now that I am in my 60's, I bless the genetics that before I had always lamented.

One afternoon I was watching the TV show Merv Griffin while I was lying on the living room floor trying to reduce the pain in my lower back. Merv had a late afternoon talk show where he interviewed celebrities. On this particular day his guest was Juliette Proust, a famous dancer and actress. Juliette was telling the audience that she kept in shape by practicing yoga. For entertainment, Merv asked her to give a demonstration. After the commercial break, she was in her unitard bending, stretching, and twisting her body into poses that looked impossible. My eyes were glued to the screen. My reaction was visceral. My whole body sighed in recognition and I thought, "Ahhh, that's what I need!"

During the next commercial break, I decided to see if there were any yoga schools near me. I walked over to the phone, got out the Yellow Pages and flipped through until I found the correct page. My fingers slid down a column until it rested on an advertisement for a yoga school that wasn't too far away. I called the number listed and received a recorded message that explained the various class times and cost. I was surprised that there was a class in a couple of hours. This was a perfect example of how synchronicity operates in your everyday life even if you are not aware of it. I didn't have to think about whether or not I would go. My body was doing all the talking and it was yelling at me to get to that class as soon as possible. I just knew I had to be there so I followed my intuition and went before I had the chance to talk myself out of it. It ended up being one of the best decisions I ever made in my life!

That night in class, everything changed. It was like I had come home and my tribe was there waiting for me! The energy that filled the room felt welcoming and loving. The instructor, Betty, a throwback to the sixties with her wrap-around peasant skirt and hair down to her waist, treated me like I was a frequent student there. Everything she said felt right and made sense to me. She made no distinction between a new student and a more advanced one. To her we were all the same. She emphasized that we should do what we could honestly and without judgment. "Look for the stretch," she kept saying. As long as you felt the stretch, the pose was being done right. What alternative universe did I fall into? I loved it.

Betty explained that the Sanskrit word "yoga" translated to English means 'to unite.' She explained further that the three components which always need to be united in perfect balance are the body, the mind, and the spirit. You cannot focus on one and not the others. In her school, she taught Hatha yoga which was the physical aspect of yoga. In class, she included a continuing dialogue on the mental and spiritual aspects to keep us balanced, which sparked my interest enough to pursue them on my own. She was a walking encyclopedia of esoteric knowledge. She even had a library in the basement of her yoga studio which she provided her students full access to. Outside of class, she offered opportunities to explore different aspects of esoteric teachings for anyone who was interested. Her offerings were always well attended.

I learned things about the body that I never knew. All movement in yoga is done with the breath. I needed to relearn how to breathe. Instead of breathing in the chest, I had to learn to breathe deep down in my solar plexus, in my lower abdomen. The mechanics of the body and how movements should be done were explained. I realized the importance of balance in strengthening muscle. When one muscle group is stronger than the antagonistic muscles, your body will be out of alignment and problems will arise. The latter was the problem with my back. I had to relax and stretch all the muscles that pull the body forward while simultaneously strengthening and tightening all the muscles that pull the body backwards. I put my focus on any pose that resulted in a backbend. For your reference, some of the poses that helped me were the table, cobra, and bridge poses. Of course, some twists like the triangle should be thrown in to loosen it all up. All of these poses can be found in books or watching videos on the internet.

Six months after starting yoga class, I was lying in bed one morning and realized I hadn't thought about my back in weeks. I was hooked for life.

Betty began and ended each class with a 15-minute meditation to help us quiet the outside world and become focused on the present moment. This was new to me. I learned there are many ways to meditate. My favorite meditation was sitting in the lotus position which was easy for me to do with my long legs. Once in position, we had to empty our minds by focusing on our breathing. Not as easy as it may seem. It brought our minds into an alpha brain state so that we could relax and center ourselves in order to focus on our poses without distraction.

By definition, meditation is quieting the mind from all thoughts and being totally focused on one thing. Betty jokingly referred to the mind as a team of runaway horses, out of control going every which way. It needed to be tamed and quieted. I have Virgo rising which causes me to overthink everything. My mind is rarely quiet. That is why I have such a hard time falling asleep at night. Meditation was definitely something I needed to master and incorporate into my daily routine in life. Drawing our attention and focus on just one thing gives our mind something to do to keep the random thoughts at bay. The most common thing to focus on is the breath. However, you can focus on anything: a candle flame, a flower, a repetitive noise like a mantra, flowing water, etc. You can literally use anything. Every time a random thought enters your consciousness, you let it go and pull your focus back to what you are meditating on. It may sound easy – give it a try! It takes just seconds for those runaway horses of the mind to go in a new direction. I can count on one hand how many times in my life that I have actually been able to do this for any length of time greater than five minutes. Those rare times are sublime! Time ceases to exist, and a sense of overwhelming calm prevails. Emptying your mind of all thoughts creates a vacuum for new ideas to flow in. Sometimes the new idea doesn't happen during the meditation, but materializes in the hours after, so don't be surprised if you are gifted with some new epiphany, understanding, creative idea, or inspiration later that day.

Guided meditations are also popular. They consist of listening to a person or a recording walk your mind through one thing at a time. An example would be a chakra meditation where the focus is on the energy centers of the etheric body one chakra at a time, beginning with the root chakra (at the base of the spine) to the crown chakra (at the top of the head). There are seven major chakras: Root, Sacral, Solar Plexus, Heart, Throat, Third Eye, and Crown. Walking through nature is another common way to be led through meditation to bring your mind into an alpha state or brainwave. Hypnotherapists use guided meditation to take your brain waves from beta to alpha and then to theta to create a mild hypnotic state where remembering and reprogramming can occur.

Meditating quickly became a daily practice for me and it still is today. In the morning, it gets me into a happy state that carries me through the day. At night it quiets my mind and empties my head of thoughts so I can release my conscious thoughts and fall asleep. Aside from reducing stress and releasing tension in the muscles, it can help you go deep within yourself to become aware of the "you of you," that eternal, energetic essence that is your soul, your higher self, your divinity. The experience is unique to each individual meditating. Whatever you choose to call it, it is all the same thing. I encourage everyone to meditate so they may discover what it is uniquely for themselves.

Many religions feel threatened by yoga and discourage its practice because it is self-empowering to go within and find your own divinity. They wish to perpetuate your dependence on an outer God that legislates what you think and can and cannot do. If we can get past religion's fear, I always think it would be wonderful to expose young children to yoga early in life so they may learn how to use and live in their bodies correctly at the beginning instead of having to relearn everything like I did later in life. It would also be of great benefit to a developing person to be in touch with the power that lies inside, prior to low-self-esteem issues developing.

Betty held group past life regressions on Friday nights. I was intrigued. Prior to my suicide attempt, I always thought life was finite; you are born, you live, and you die. I was aware that some philosophies embrace the soul as eternal, living lifetime after lifetime, but I could not accept that. It went against my fantasy of suicide as an escape. I had envisioned that my moment of death was going to be the last thing I was feeling, then blessed nothingness. No heaven and no hell. After all, my goal of suicide was the ultimate release into nothingness. If we reincarnated, what would be the point? We would just have to come back and do it all over again. But mysteriously, the day after my suicide attempt, I suddenly referred to my next life. Where did that knowledge come from? I can only guess that I always knew, I just needed to be reminded of it. Since I decided to stick around on Earth, I thought it would be great to get confirmation on the possibility of reincarnation. The following Friday night, I found myself lying on the floor with about ten other people. I was comfortable and relaxed because I was in the room where we took yoga classes. It had become a safe haven for me and I didn't feel threatened in any way.

Past life? Bring it on.

Without much ado, Betty, the yoga instructor, explained what was going to happen so we would know what to expect and what to do after the regression. While lying on the floor, she would first take us into a meditative state using a guided meditation that would eventually get us to a mild hypnotic state. Once she got us into a safe place, she was going to take us through a door that would open up to another life that we had enjoyed. Not one that would freak us out. That would be for a therapist to orchestrate. Once we were in a past life, she would go through a list of key phrases to help us experience that life. For example, she would ask questions such as: What are you wearing? Where do you get your supplies? What was the lesson learned? To end the regression, she would have us disassociate from the past life and view it in the third person perspective so she could guide us through how we died without being emotionally triggered by the experience. After the regression, she asked us to be quiet and not speak in order to provide an opportunity to write down everything we could remember. Prior to the regression, she handed out a sheet of paper with the key phrases on it with which to prompt our memory of the experience. She would give us time to write down whatever we could recollect from the past life we had just remembered. Once everybody was done writing, we would go around the room and share our experiences. It all sounded so simple for such an unusual endeavor.

The regression took around thirty minutes. I easily went into a mild hypnotic state. My door opened unto a life where I was a swashbuckler on a Spanish galleon docked at a thriving seaport town. Apparently, I was involved in trading, moving goods from port to port along the Mediterranean coasts in the 1400s, give or take a hundred years. It must have been prosperous for me because I was dressed in a fancy, flamboyant, brocade coat, and a huge, feathered hat on my head with a sword hanging from my waist. It was wild and fun with a lot of time spent in taverns filled with bawdy barmaids to have romantic adventures with. When Betty directed us to float up and look down to witness how we died (without any emotional attachment), I saw that I was in a sword fight aboard a ship that was still anchored at port. A sword went through my chest. In that moment of death, I very plainly remembered thinking to myself something to the effect of, "Well, I knew that would be my end given my lifestyle". I was surprisingly okay with my demise.

There was nothing special about my swashbuckler life. It didn't seem to have any relevance to my current life except that I love anything to do with water and boats, especially sailing and have been known to be flamboyant in dress from time to time. However, the experience of remembering it all was profound. During the past life regression, the minute Betty asked about one of the key phrases, I instantly knew the answer or saw it in my surroundings. There wasn't any time for my mind to be making it up. It was like it was actually happening to me. I could feel, smell, and hear everything that was going on. I can't say it was like watching a movie because I wasn't a spectator. I was in the brocade coat and feathered hat as everything unfolded around me. I would've needed a mirror to see what my face looked like. The experience left me with no doubt that this did happen. If anybody wanted to argue with me about the validity of the experience when I shared it, I would say, "You have the experience first, then we'll talk."

It was interesting to hear what other people remembered in their past life regression when we went around the room. Most people went to a past life in our planet's history such as during the Egyptian times. Nobody recalled being someone prominent. Most were poor existences, and I recall one as being wealthy. One person didn't remember anything but felt unusually relaxed after the meditation. There were two that were really surprising. They both went into the future. At the time, I didn't think that was a possibility but now I understand that time is a man-made construct to help us experience life, but in reality, everything is happening simultaneously in the magic moment of the present. One had an experience as if she were in the Jetsons' cartoon with very advanced technology doing everything for her. While the other was an inter galactic in a spaceship flying around through the universe. Betty made a joke after everybody in the group shared that the most boring past life remembrances were the ones that happened on the prairie in pioneering days because all they did was sit and watch the grass grow and the clouds float by.

After the experience of the past life regression, I realized I must have been a yogi in past lives. When I saw Juliet Prowse in her unitard doing her yoga demonstration on the Merv Griffin show, on some level, I must have recalled yoga from a previous life. That would explain why I jumped into it so quickly without giving it any thought. Why I had such a strong affinity for it and why I picked it up so readily. For me it was a process of remembering. It was mind boggling how much I, and my life, had changed in the year following seeing that show.

I only attended two additional past life regressions. The novelty wore off pretty quickly. I successfully tried regressing myself while I was lying in the sun, one of my favorite things to do, a few times. I followed the meditation Betty used in her regressions to the letter except when I came to the part to direct my remembrance to a specific life. I guided myself to a life that helped me understand what was happening in my present life or to a life that I had shared with a person in this life to help me understand what role they were playing or what issue we were trying to work out. It turned out to be a useful tool I could utilize anytime to help understand my current experience. I even added past life regression to the services I offered through my massage and healing businesses.

Meditation and past life regressions exposed me to hypnosis and the power of the subconscious mind. The subconscious mind is a storehouse of information absorbed over lifetimes and forms beliefs, vows, contracts, imprints, programs, and patterns that we are not consciously aware of. Without our knowing, they control what does and does not happen in our everyday lives.

The example I use in my healing work is the creation of a vow. Here is an example of how that would work. Say, I have a woman in her forties sitting in front of me. She wants to know why love and marriage have eluded her throughout her life. As I energetically researched what the origin of the issue may be, I discovered that her first and only love happened when she was sixteen and it ended badly and caused her pain. Her response to the pain was anger - one of the most powerful of emotions. In her anger, at sixteen, she vowed never to leave herself open to that kind of pain ever again. She unknowingly created a vow to avoid love so she wouldn't have to experience a painful breakup again. That vow got stored in her subconscious and it affected the rest of her life. My job as a healer was to release that vow so it would no longer be a block to finding love in her life.

I employed a Hypnotherapist in my early thirties to quit smoking. I smoked heavily as a teenager then quit when I was 21 when I got involved in bodybuilding. I was good for a couple of years until a long-term relationship that I was in ended. I found myself going out dancing a lot and enjoying my new found freedom. It is easy to feel lonely in a crowded bar after having somebody at my side for so long. I started bumming cigarettes off people as a way to meet them. It didn't take long for the habit to return. I became a social smoker. If I went out, I had to have a cigarette which by the end of the evening totaled an entire pack. Of course, I had trouble the next few days at the gym trying to breathe. My work outs were so important to me, I was determined to quit again. Not that easy this time around. I struggled for ten years trying to shake the habit. I would go for weeks, even months at a time without a smoke, but I would always end up lighting up again. I finally admitted I needed help. I found myself a hypnotherapist.

The Hypnotherapist interviewed me to find out what all my triggers were then regressed me to the time in my life when smoking became attractive to me. She then gave me hypnotic suggestions to counter that experience and eradicate my desire to smoke. To reinforce my resolve not to smoke, in the form of hypnotic suggestions, she reprogramed my subconscious mind and how it responded to smoking. For example, when I saw somebody light up, which was one of my triggers, I would get nauseous at the thought of lighting up myself. There were many other hypnotic suggestions she blessed me with but I won't list them here. The end result was that I no longer smoked.

The results were so miraculous, I went back and had her work on my driving habits. I was always getting speeding tickets and was consistently one ticket away from getting my license suspended. She went through the same process and what she uncovered still amazes me. Apparently, I became addicted to speed when I was a kid winning all my races on the swim team. It was the first time in my life I got positive accolades for anything. The experience was so powerful it imprinted my subconscious with the need to be fast. I still hear the hypnotic suggestions she blessed me with. Whenever I'm driving, I remind myself I am not in a race and I don't have to be first. I stopped getting speeding tickets.

Embracing reincarnation changed everything for me. It expanded my reality and understanding to a much larger view of the human experience and how I fit into it. First, suicide was not really an option anymore. Even though it's still a familiar 'go-to' place when I was depressed and feeling hopeless, I knew it would not be the smartest choice. I now understand that what I don't achieve in this lifetime, I will have to do it again in subsequent lives until I learn the lesson I'm struggling with. Learning this shaped my commitment to be the best I can be in this life so I will be further ahead in the next, and hopefully stronger.

The principle of reincarnation is the keystone in making sense of many of the philosophies and religions of our world. How is a human supposed to achieve enlightenment and evolve to their divinity all in one life? It is just not possible. We learn and grow through our experiences and mistakes. Sometimes we have to make the same mistake numerous times until we get it right and can move on. One lesson may take many lifetimes. Other times we master many lessons in one lifetime. What we bring into a life is contingent on what we learned in all of our previous incarnations. It is all accumulating, bringing us closer to the soul's goal of reuniting with source, the divine, God... however you wish to define or label your higher power. It blows my mind and makes me calm and happy all at the same time. Knowing life has meaning and purpose makes it much more palatable than if this life is random and it's all there is. It is also nice to know that we are infinite beings that never die. We just change forms and bodies as needed. I get excited just thinking about what I want to be and do in my next life.

Many religions and philosophies require that you have faith. Faith that it is all happening as it should. Faith to accept the divine mystery. As I learn and evolve, my mind keeps expanding to the immensity of it all. Humans on Earth are only a pinprick of experience that is going on in the universe and beyond. I know we are only using a small portion of our brains, but even if we were using it to its full capacity, I think there are some things we don't have the ability to assimilate. For instance, the one concept I cannot fathom is that the number of lives we can lead is infinite and that they are cyclical. For me that takes faith. It's too big for me to truly understand so I put that in the category of 'divine mystery.' Just because I can't understand something doesn't make it false. There is a lot going on in science that I don't understand but there is quantitative evidence to support theories. I choose to navigate through the unknown or incomprehensible with faith.

I think this would be a good time to discuss the concept of relativity in comparing one thing to another. I believe we live many lives so we can experience all possibilities and thus be informed to make the ultimate choice of accepting our divine holiness. Holiness as in whole or at one with everything. As humans, we are given free will to make that choice. I don't believe it is possible to blindly make a choice of such immense magnitude on what we are told in any one doctrine. Our free will guides us to the experiences we need to have in order to learn about them so we can make a well-informed choice. We need the positive and negative of the experience to understand what is at stake and then we can choose accordingly.

I remember in eighth grade science class when I was introduced to the concept of relativity. The teacher, Mrs. Winkle, set up three buckets of water, each at a different temperature. I volunteered to stick my hand in a bucket and report if the water was hot or cold. I did as I was told and reported that the water was hot. She had me put my hand in the next bucket. That felt even hotter. She then directed me to put my hand back in the original bucket. Now, after experiencing the second hot bucket of water, the first felt cold. How could the first bucket be both hot and cold? The lesson here was that you can't define one thing without knowing the relationship with the things around it. Nothing is absolute. Everything is being affected by what is around it.

In life, we need to experience one thing in order to know and understand another thing. We can't know what light is until we understand what dark is. How do you define good if you don't know what evil is? Fast or slow, young or old, male and female, good and bad, etc. We are given an infinite number of lives to figure it all out. Only after many lifetimes of experience can we truly exercise our free will to choose the Divine.

———————————————

B etty's biggest gift to me, thou she probably didn't know it, was my participation the Harmonic Convergence. This momentous event enabled what is happening right now in 2024 and the transformation the planet is going through.

Betty was a mover and shaker in the New Age spiritual community. She was always gathering people into groups for one kind of meditation or another. She explained it was more powerful to meditate in a group because the power generated went exponential to the number of people meditating. So, if there were ten people meditating together, the power generated would be ten to the tenth power. When you do the math that comes out to ten billion. WOW! To put it another way, when ten people meditate together, the power they generate is the same as ten billion people meditating separately.

Betty had an advanced understanding of astrology and referred to it often. She wanted to know my birth date and time so she could do my astrological natal chart and see how I fit into her life. After she looked at my chart, I remember her saying that I would be a great teacher's assistant. She had piqued my interest in astrology which is when I started researching and reading books to learn more.

I first heard about the Harmonic Convergence when Betty started talking about an astrological event that happened only once every ten thousand years. Planets were going to line up in such a way that would cause a portal to open, letting in a wave of love to fuel a spiritual awakening that would cause a global shift to enlightenment and pave the way for the end of the old paradigm. A new age would slowly emerge on the planet that would personify peace, harmony, and empathy called the Golden Age on Earth. I had read about the coming of the Golden Age before so even though I was new to all this, it made sense. Where we lived in Cleveland, it was going to happen on August 16th, 1987 at 6:00 am.

Betty's enthusiasm and excitement were contagious. Even though I wasn't a morning person, I committed to participating. Betty spearheaded a drive to organize a meditation event and to get people to it. The meditation had to occur at a high vibrational site. Where we lived, that was the beach. One of my favorite places! I got so involved, I designed and printed flyers that I took with me and posted wherever I went. People were organizing all over the world. There were 200 official meditating sites in the United States alone. I don't know who the big organizers were, but I heard that in order to tip the scales into the new paradigm, 104,000 people needed to be meditating at the exact same time globally. Remember what I said about the power created by a group meditating together at the same time? The power of it will be exponentially increased by the number of people meditating. I can't even do the math to figure out the power that would be created if they actually got that many people to participate. As the day grew closer, I became more excited. I had never done anything like this before.

I'm going to pause here and chart exactly what happened in the heavens astrologically for anybody who may be interested. If you are not, please skip ahead.

The Sun, Mercury, Venus, and Mars were conjunct in the sun of Leo, a highly creative fire sign. A conjunction is when the planets line up right on top of each other. Fire signs are all about high creative energy. This conjunction was trined by Jupiter in Aries, with Saturn and Uranus in Sagittarius, two more fire signs. A trine is a positive empowering aspect. These six planets and the Moon formed a Grand Trine that created the harmonic flow of energy that was to bring humanity into a new age of spiritual enlightenment. Of course, at the time, this didn't mean much to me.

I pulled an all-nighter to make sure I was on the beach that morning at 6:00 am. At least a hundred people showed up. There wasn't any fanfare. Most of us stood in a circle and meditated to bring in the new energy for twenty minutes and then it was over. Betty emphasized what an important moment in time this was and how important it was that we were all there. When it was over, she thanked us all for making the effort to show up and be there for humanity. When I was walking up the hill to the parking lot, I overheard people sharing stories of their experiences while in meditation; crystals vibrating in pockets, voices speaking, the intensity of the energy, and colors. I didn't experience anything out of the ordinary. Admittedly, I felt slightly euphoric from meditating, but nothing mystical. I went home and went to bed.

At the next yoga class, Betty reported that the number of people meditating worldwide greatly exceeded expectations, going well over the critical number to reach the needed tipping point. The portal was opened and the Earth plane started receiving new powerful energies that would awaken people to their own power, the connection with the Divine, and the God within which is the core tenant of spirituality. This allows us to go within for answers instead of looking outward.

Everything that was ever learned is residing inside of us waiting to be remembered. In conversation, I've learned to differentiate between religion and spirituality by explaining that religion teaches to look outside of yourself for God, up in the heavens or a man-made temple. Spirituality teaches us to go inward because God lives in all human beings. There is a greeting in many eastern philosophies that we use in yoga. It is "Namaste" which means the Divine in me bows to the Divine in you coming from the Hindu belief that God resides in everyone, so every person you greet deserves the respect accorded to God. We are all extensions of God which implies that we are all one. That is why it is said that what you do for yourself, you do for everybody. It makes you think twice when making decisions about how to treat people.

We congratulated ourselves and moved on.

I pretty much forgot about the Harmonic Convergence until COVID-19 in 2020 and the Insurrection in 2021 when things really started to happen with the transition energy we had been experiencing since 2012 that has sped up the move into the Aquarian age. The latter couldn't have happened without the former. The Harmonic Convergence opened up the portal for the transformative energy to flow in. I didn't put it all together until it became obvious that the energy on Earth was changing in the first two decades of the new millennia. I then realized what an honor it was to have had the opportunity to be a part of the Harmonic Convergence, a pivotal moment in our evolution. I think it is interesting that I had my personal spiritual awakening the year before. This ensured I would hear about the Harmonic Convergence *and* be open to participating in the opening of the portal which ushered in the energy fueling the transition into the new age. It feeds into my belief that I purposefully incarnated when I did to be a facilitator in the transition.

Betty asked me to stop attending class after a couple of years. She said I was making other students uncomfortable with my enthusiasm and ability. She recognized that I was too much in my ego and I needed to get out of it. I was angry and disappointed because yoga class was my sanctuary. I continued to do daily yoga on my own. Doing it alone was a totally different experience. There was nothing to distract me which enabled me to go inward. There was no adulation for a pose well done. It was purely for myself. It surprised me how deeply I would get into a pose and the stretch was much more intense. Betty was right, with no teacher or class to impress, I began to do yoga for myself without ego.

Yoga has facilitated having a problem free body that remains youthful till this day. Betty was not only an excellent instructor of yoga; she blessed me with the tools to deeply explore and understand my spirituality and divinity. To be what I remembered in every moment of my journey. In class, I was exposed to many things I wasn't aware of. I learned how to be still and quiet my mind with meditation. Through past life regression I learned that we are eternal souls living lifetime after lifetime and that all the information from those lives is omnipresent and easy to access through hypnosis. She made me aware of the energy systems of the body and the seven major chakras. And, that our physicality is at the center of an immense energy vortex that is called an aura. When we come in contact with somebody, the first thing we are picking up is their aura which communicates to the receiver who they are and what their intentions are. That is often why we find ourselves attracted to certain people and not others. I met wonderful people in class that expanded my understanding through their company, conversation, book referrals, and seminars. Betty also provided me with an opportunity to participate in changing the world we live in energetically and an awareness of the transformational age that we are experiencing. It was through her that I was able to start putting it all together. I thank Betty and yoga often when I do my gratitude list. I owe her so much of who I am.

The time I spent in Betty's yoga class and all the people I encountered there in those two years taught me that we are multifaceted beings. Our physicality is just a part of our experience. We have a conscious awareness that thinks. We call it the mind. Most people think that the mind resides in our brain but we think with our entire bodies, especially our heart. We have an external soul of pure energy that we call our spirit body. Spirit uses the mind to imagine what it wants to create, and our physicality is the experience of our creation. We need all three. We also need all three to heal and evolve. Everything that happens shows up in all three bodies. If the mind doesn't process emotion, which is energy, associated with an experience then it gets stored in the body and may become the root cause for a disease. We ultimately can't cure something until we get in touch with the root cause of the problem and let it go. I try to let my emotions flow in the moment so that nothing gets stored. For emotions that are already stored, I utilize an energetic healer like myself to get in touch with and release the energy. I have also noticed that if we put all our intention into one of the three, we cannot help but affect the other two. For example, for most of my twenties I was all about bodybuilding. It turned out that working out was very meditative and opened up my mind to other things. Some of my best ideas have come during workouts at the gym. I've often said that my bodybuilding opened me up to my spirituality and yoga. Yoga in turn put me in touch with all the disease in my body that needed to be healed, which in turn, enhanced my performance with the weights at the gym. Insight, epiphanies, and connection come after yoga and meditation. Spirit goes along for the ride whatever you do because, after all, that is the essence of who we are. I love the fact that bodybuilding and yoga are at opposite ends of the spectrum. One is very aggressive and the other is the definition of passive. Between the two I have a wonderful balance point somewhere in the middle. The end goal is always a perfect balance between the body, the mind, and spirit.

N AMASTE!

Setting Intentions

It was customary for me to take a long walk on the beach every day if possible. I remember one particular day in my mid-twenties. It was a beautiful, sunny day with a cool breeze blowing, tickling the surface of the water creating a barely audible soft crash of surf hitting the shore. Just the kind of day that puts me into a dreamy mood. I found myself fantasizing about what I would do if I was gifted with three wishes. I contemplated various options in my head but nothing felt right.

Even though I played the lottery with the hope of winning big one day, I quickly discarded the obvious dream of wealth as not all that important. What could be more desirable than wealth? I kept thinking if I really, really had three wishes, I wanted to do something big to change the world and make it a better place for everybody. Personal wealth seemed like a waste of a wish compared to that. I expanded my ruminations to things that would have a positive effect on mankind and the world. That felt much better and the ideas instantly began to flow. For the first wish I settled on ending all war on the planet. Growing up in the shadow of the Vietnam War and watching all the pain and suffering it caused every day on the evening news, made peace on the planet a top priority for me. The idea of all nations and religions living in peace felt really good. What next? I started thinking about other causes of pain and suffering on the planet. What is the greatest cause of it? My mind flashed on diseases. AIDS was just beginning to wreak its havoc on the world causing people to suffer and die in unimaginable pain. Ah-ha! Second wish:

Cure all disease in the world. Keeping with the theme of what causes pain and suffering, I decided my third wish was to eliminate world hunger. I reflected on my choices. If all those things came to pass, what a wonderful world we would live in. Truly, a place I wouldn't mind sticking around and enjoying. I have to admit I was rather proud of my selfless philanthropy.

After that walk on the beach, the desire to be able to cure all diseases continued to be on my mind. For some reason, that resonated the strongest with me. I easily pictured myself as a modern-day Jesus Christ with the ability to lay my hands on somebody who was suffering and make them well. There was a part of me that knew, without question, that the ability to heal energetically was more than just stories in a book, but a real possibility. Later, after I began my spiritual journey, I read of many instances throughout history when people had the gift to do just that. I figured if they could do it, so could I. The idea of becoming a healer went from fantasy to, "How can I make this happen?"

Along with curing the sick, I wanted to create a better world. I loved reading about utopian societies where everybody was taken care of and treated equally because diversity was celebrated instead of being marginalized. A place where there was no violence or crime because there wasn't any poverty. A planet that was well tended for because everyone knew the importance of protecting the sphere that supported their existence. The environment would be naturally breathtaking at every turn. It was a wonderful vision that did not coincide with the reality of the day. I intuitively knew it shouldn't be the way that it was currently, on Earth. What had happened to make it this way? What could we do to effect positive change?

Careful what you think about. I didn't know it at the time, but I was setting an intention.

I met Gabe on my annual camping trip to Cape Cod in 1989. He was working as a massage therapist in the small seaside town that I was staying in. We met while we were walking to the beach to enjoy the perfectly hot, sunny afternoon. My towel fell out of my beach bag without me noticing. Gabe was behind me, saw that I was ignorant of my loss, picked up the towel and ran to catch up to me. I was deep in thought and his sudden presence at my side startled me. He apologized for surprising me and handed me my towel while explaining that it fell out of my bag. I overcame my confusion and thanked him for his thoughtfulness. We fell into step with one another and started talking. It was quickly apparent that we shared the same spiritual beliefs and views of the world. We spent the afternoon sharing my blanket and catching a tan while trading stories and ideas. By the time the sun started its descent to the horizon, we were fast friends.

I ended up hanging out with him as much as I could whenever he wasn't working giving people massages. It was a treat for me to find somebody I could talk to openly about the new world I was discovering and not be worried about being judged as a weirdo because of who I was and what I believed in. He was a gentle soul brimming with empathy and well wishes for his fellow man. He had gravitated to becoming a massage therapist because he saw his life as one of service. He took great joy in helping alleviate people's stress, helping them to heal and bringing pleasure to those who sought him out for a massage. He had my full attention!

He was surprised that I had never had a massage. It surprised me as well, given the fact that my mother had trained all of her children to massage her back in the evenings while she lay on the floor and watched television. She loved putting her kids to work. Once she quipped that the only reason, she had children was so she would have somebody to do her dishes. We believed her. Gabe, very generously offered to give me my first professional massage as a gift. I couldn't say no to that!

The next afternoon, instead of going to the beach, he came to my campsite and set up his table under the shade of the pine trees. The camp site never looked better. He quickly relieved my awkwardness by instructing me on how he wanted me to lie on the table. I did as I was told while he put on a cassette tape of relaxing music. I was a little nervous, but after the first few strokes, I gave into the moment and surrendered. I had never experienced anything like it before. The loving touch of Gabe's hands transported me to another time and place. I forgot about everything! I felt like I was gently floating on the warm, soft breeze among the fragrant pines. It was one of the most wonderful experiences I had ever had. I was so relaxed and in the moment that I fell fast asleep. Gabe had to shake me awake to let me know he was done. I was incredulous that a whole hour had gone by. It seemed like he had just begun. I slowly sat up forcing my muscles into action. When my eyes met Gabe's, I shook my head in sleepy wonder. I could barely utter how much I enjoyed it. He quietly stood there knowingly. I could see why he was making money so readily. I would pay to have that done to me anytime. I was hooked. That afternoon changed my life.

My two weeks on Cape Cod always flew by way too quickly, but meeting Gabe this year made that an understatement. It seemed like I had just met him and now I had to say goodbye. I was going to miss my new friend. I wanted to take him home with me for a multitude of reasons, but some things are not meant to be. He had a life in Maryland that he would return to after the season was over and I would become a fond memory of his summer.

It was a twelve-hour drive home which gave me plenty of time to reflect on my vacation, my new friend, and massage therapy. It did not escape my attention that Gabe was different like me. It was the glue of our friendship. But, unlike me, instead of working at a job where he didn't fit in, he created his own career where being different was an advantage and not an obstacle and he was making a lot of money in the process. At the time, I was working a low paying job that I dreaded going to each day. I really admired his courage to strike out from the norm and create his own business. There is a lot to be said for being an entrepreneur. I was still full of positive energy from my vacation, and I suddenly thought if Gabe could do it his way, then so could I! With each passing mile, I became more and more convinced that becoming a massage therapist would be the perfect fit for me. I caught my reflection in the rearview mirror and was surprised that I was smiling from ear-to-ear. Just the thought of doing it was making me happy. I started to make a plan.

As soon as the car was unpacked, I was thumbing through the Yellow Pages for a massage school. I found one! It took just one minute to get somebody on the phone. I found out the fall session was going to start on Saturday. Talk about perfect timing! The program would take a year going to classes on Saturday from 8:00 am to 8:00 pm with one weekend off between each of the four semesters. By the end of the conversation, I was enrolled. Their schedule was perfect. I could still work my forty-hour week and go to school full time. The schedule would be grueling! Once my mind is made up, I do whatever it takes to succeed. Saturday, at eight in the morning, I showed up with a check in hand to start my new career as a Licensed Massage Therapist.

It made my head spin how fast it all happened. For me, when the Universe is moving me towards my destiny, it happens lightning quick. I get hit with divine inspiration, I pursue it, and everything falls perfectly into place. It reminded me of how I ended up in a yoga class hours after I first learned that yoga even existed. I have noticed that when things fall easily into place for me that confirms

I'm moving in the right direction. Massage school was definitely the right direction.

I knew from the first day I sat in class that I would become a successful therapist and that this was how I was going to make a living. The curriculum was intense given we only met once a week from eight in the morning to eight at night. I had to memorize the thousand-page anatomy book along with massage theory, the mechanics of massage, diseases of the body, and legal courses tossed in. I was extremely lucky that I worked evenings at a job that only took me a couple of hours to do, allowing me the remainder of the shift to study. When I was in university the first time, I was lucky to have even a 2.5 grade point average because I was so unmotivated. I had no direction. In massage school I maintained a grade point average of 4.0 all four semesters. Even I was impressed by how dedicated I was.

Upon graduation, I had to pass a two-day State Medical Board Exam. In the state of Ohio, a Massage Therapist licensure was an official medical license just like becoming a registered nurse. When the results came in the mail, I stared at the envelope from the state board for a long time before I found the courage to open it. Inside held the fate of my future. I can't say I aced it, but I was in the 87th percentile. Something to be proud of given how intense the testing was. I stood in my kitchen and cried with relief and happiness.

It took me six months to segue from the job I couldn't stand to doing to massage full time. Once it was obvious that the money was going to be good enough to support myself, I took the leap, quit my job, and became self-employed. For a hot minute I considered working for somebody in a clinical environment but that meant I would have to follow a schedule, work eight hours, and deal with medical rehabilitation issues. None of which I wanted to do. Being self-employed meant that I could make my own hours, limit the number of massages in a day so as to not put too much stress on my hands, and do the kind of massage that I liked doing. Also, I got to set my own fee and keep 100% of the profits!

I was on call seven days a week from noon to midnight. I was one of the first people I knew to carry a clunky cell phone strapped around my waist in a fanny pack. A client could come to me, or I would go to them; "have a table, will travel" was my motto. I would do a max of four massages in a day. I quickly found out if I did more than four, I would wake up in the middle of the night and my hands would be numb. That scared me a little. What if there was a fire and I couldn't grasp a door knob to open and escape. The only exception was when I was hired to do a wedding party that had more than four people. Wedding parties always tipped well. They were worth a little pain and suffering. All in all, limiting myself to four massages a day ended up being a good decision. My hands lasted longer in the business than anybody else that I knew.

I was lucky in the beginning to happen to be in the right place at the right time knowing some well-connected people. Satisfied clients told their friends about my work, then those people told their friends, etc. I also knew someone who worked the box office at Playhouse Square, the theater complex in downtown Cleveland. He got my name on the fact sheet that was handed out to cast and crew for services they may need while in town. I ended up massaging some famous people. And, one of the perks of working with the theater crowd was complimentary show tickets. If the entertainers didn't know anyone to give them too, they would ask if I wanted them. I never refused. Finally, I ran a classified ad in the local art and entertainment magazine which provided me with a lot of out-of-towners on business trips. Sometimes, that ad attracted bizarre people, but no job is perfect. Between the three, I was as busy as I wanted to be. When I look back on how easily it all fell into place for me, I realize that my absolute knowing at the beginning of school that I would be a success helped me as a co-creator with the universe to bring it into reality. It all played out perfectly. I was successfully self-employed doing a job I loved and making good money. I was living the dream.

Massage is something you never stop learning about. Of course, there is nothing like experience to teach you, but there are an endless number of styles and therapies one could pursue if inclined. I chose to learn about the Alternative Medicine modalities that work with the energy flow in the body. Humans are so much more than what the eye can see or what shows up in a MRI. My dream of becoming someone who could heal by touch was becoming a reality. One of my clients who couldn't afford to get massages as frequently as he wanted suggested we barter. I bartered for many things over the years. He was a Reiki Master. He offered to teach me reiki and do my attunements in exchange for massages. I readily agreed. Before long I was a Reiki Master. I was always aware that I had a strong flow of energy emanating from my hands. I could turn it on and off. I would showboat for friends and have them put their hands on mine so they could feel it go on and off. Because of yoga, I was aware that we are energetic beings and energy can be directed for healing. Now with reiki, I had a system I could channel it through to amplify and direct it. I always contributed part of my success to my naturally inherent good touch and to that flow of energy. That's not something you can learn in a class. A person either has it or they don't. After that, my clients not only received a massage from me, they also received an energetic healing.

Another friend of mine was pursuing Polarity Therapy, which sparked my interest. This employs working with the magnetic fields of the body. The body is a magnet just like planet Earth is with a north and south pole. Positive energy flows up the right side of the body and flows down the left. The right hand is positive and sends energy. The left hand is negative and receives energy. Also, there are five waves of energy flowing around the body at all times. Disease can occur when an energy flow is out of balance. A polarity therapist uses their respective hands to re-balance the flow of energies and restore homeostasis back to the body. Polarity work became a part of my arsenal in doing my healing work. I also incorporated traditional eastern medicines like Acupressure, (acupuncture without the needles), Shiatsu, and Reflexology all of which work with the energy centers and the flow of energy through the body. All of these dove-tailed beautifully with the belief system I embraced from my yoga practice. Everything I learned confirmed my original belief that we are all of one divine energy.

Massage is a very intimate experience. A client really has to trust the therapist in order to lay on the table naked and leave themselves open enough to let go and relax. A good therapist has a warm, friendly, accepting personality and their calming, peaceful energy should put people at ease as soon as they walk into the room. Their touch should immediately be able to communicate love and healing. I innately possess these qualities. I believe that is the reason many of my regulars ended up being good friends of mine. I often found myself in the position of confidant and counselor. Clients would open up to me while they were on the table and share what was going on in their lives and the problems they were running into. Of course, their stories often seemed to end with question marks like they were expecting me to offer them some sage wisdom or advice. Most people just need to hear some good common sense for clarification. Maybe it's easier to see solutions to problems when they are somebody else's and not your own. In any event, I always did my best to offer what I felt was appropriate. I found myself pulling a lot from my spiritual beliefs. So many people end up being brainwashed by their culture, religion, or society that they forget how to think for themselves. What seemed obvious to me was totally alien to them. I always encourage looking outside of the box and seeing things from another perspective.

The following is a short list of the spiritual beliefs I accrued over the years that I would share when needed:

We are here to learn. Look for the lesson to give your experience meaning.

We are all one. How would you like it if somebody did that to you?

Don't make assumptions.

Don't judge. What is right for one might not be right for somebody else.

Nobody can legislate morality. There is no right or wrong.

The only place you have any power is in your own backyard.

If we don't have any power over it, let it go.

Everything happens for a reason.

Always trust your intuition.

Recognize and let go of ego. Your own or somebody else's, or both.

It takes two to play a game. If you walk away the game ceases to exist.

Follow your heart and passion.

You are the master of your experience creating it moment by moment.

ESCAPING MADNESS

Be mindful of your thoughts, actions, and beliefs.

Live in truth. Don't tell lies and don't accept other people's dishonesty.

It's okay to fuck up, everybody does at one time or another.

Live in love. Send love to whoever and wherever it is needed.

Bad actions beget bad actions.

Like energies attract so be in a place of positivity at all times.

Always do what you want as long as it doesn't hurt somebody else in the process.

Do what's right for you, not somebody else. Always be true to yourself.

Take care of yourself, your wants and needs come first.

Happiness comes from within; nobody can make you happy.

If you're not happy, you have nothing to share with others.

Most of these sound like common sense but it is surprising how many people need to be reminded - we all do. Much later I realized that what I was doing was trusting my intuition and letting whatever came to my mind flow to my clients. I tried to be in the moment. I never said what I thought they wanted to hear, I said what I thought would be most helpful to bring peace and happiness into their lives even if it may have made them or myself uncomfortable. At the end of a session, clients would thank me for being open and honest and generally exclaimed that I told them just what they needed to hear!

Sometimes, I spontaneously responded to a situation or problem with counsel that I didn't realize I knew. Once I talked for about twenty minutes, amazing myself as well as my client with the wisdom and understanding that came out of my mouth. When I was done, I took a deep breath and continued my body work but, in my head, I was thinking, "Where the hell did that just come from?" That was not an isolated event. I noticed it was beginning to happen more frequently and not just while I was doing massage. It took me a while to realize that I was so well connected with my higher self and source energy that I was gifted in the moment with whatever needed to be communicated to best serve my client or friend. I didn't feel like I was channeling. For me channeling is when an entity steps in and talks through a person. It was more like a door was opening to things I already knew but had forgotten. And, suddenly it was instantly available for me to share with whomever needed to hear it.

I keep using the word "remembering" because in my present, I now understand that as an infinite soul I already know everything. When a human incarnates, a veil covers up everything in the higher dimensions to give a soul an opportunity to use their freewill to attract them to experiences they need in order to learn and make better choices going forward. Ultimately, that will cause them to remember what their soul has known all along. I think, in my case, the veil was on the thin side because I started remembering stuff early and swiftly.

I n my mid-thirties, I suffered from a health issue that spanned over three years. I had no energy and my bowels were mush. I couldn't

figure out what was going on. I went to a couple of medical doctors in the beginning and after countless tests, they came up empty handed. The second one, just to be safe, put me on a heavy-duty antibiotic called Flagyl. That really sent my bowels south. I was at my wits end. I didn't know what to do.

Someone told me about an energetic healer people had phenomenal experiences with. I was so desperate, I thought, "What is there to lose?" So, I gave her a try. Her work was powerful. I could actually feel her pushing and pulling energy in, out, and around without ever touching me. I felt totally recharged by the time she was done working on me. When she was finished, she told me I had candida. I must have had a confused look on my face because she asked me if I knew what that was. I replied, "A vaginal yeast infection." She laughed and explained that in my case it was systemic. Apparently, yeast is normally present in your digestive tract. The Flagyl had killed all the good flora in my intestines allowing the yeast to take over. She told me to stay away from anything with yeast in it. That helped for a short time but after a while my constant fatigue returned. It was so bad I would go to the gym to work out, and leave after a couple of exercises because I didn't have the energy to finish. I would go home, crawl into bed, and cry. I was so frustrated. I wasn't living life the way I wanted to.

I started to hear from my massage clients about a new doctor in town that was performing miracles. One had her allergies eliminated and another's scoliosis was dramatically improved. His name was Dr. Keith Jordan. I immediately recognized the name. He had a classified ad in the newspaper I read with his picture. He was a newly graduated Chiropractor and was in the early stages of establishing himself. Every time I saw the ad, I would linger on it looking at his picture. There was something about him… I don't know why, but I didn't follow up or make an appointment with him. I think maybe it sounded too good to be true. I don't know. In retrospect, I realize that my intuition was trying to guide me to go but I didn't know enough then to pay attention to that guidance. I know now to always watch what catches your attention and where your mind is going because it is usually leading you somewhere.

My condition got so extreme that I started getting sick all the time. I would get over one virus and catch another one a few days later. I was getting everything that came down the viral pipeline. After months of this, I woke up one morning in a state of complete surrender and desperation. I crawled out of bed and pulled the latest edition of the newspaper out of the trash. I found the chiropractor's ad and called the number. I was sitting on his exam table an hour later. At this point I was looking for a miracle.

Dr. Keith, as he liked to be called, asked all the important questions while I blurted out my story. I think I was crying. He told me to raise my outstretched arm perpendicular to my body in front of me while holding it strong. He programmed my body to hold the arm strong for a 'no' response and to go weak for a 'yes' response just by asking my innate, the divine intelligence of the body, to respond in those ways. He explained it was a way for him to communicate with my body. He called muscle testing. It was part of a system he learned at school called Total Body Modification. This was all new to me. He started mumbling questions and pushing down on my arm after each one. My arm would hold strong and not move for a 'no' response and to my surprise, my arm would fall down out of sheer weakness for a 'yes' response. Regardless of how hard I tried, I couldn't keep my arm up. It was like a poltergeist had taken over my body. After a few minutes of talking to my body, Dr. Keith took a step back, looked me in the eye, and told me I had parasites in every organ of my body. Because of that, my immune system was so weak from fighting the parasites that it was practically non-functional and that is why I was catching one virus after another. I sat there dumb founded! He gleaned all that after a few minutes of muscle testing?

Other doctors had done all kinds of tests which had taken weeks to get results back and came up with nothing. It was a relief to finally have someone tell me definitively what was wrong with my body. He may have come to the diagnosis in an unusual way but what he said seemed right. On some level it all made sense to me. At that moment, I put all my trust and faith in him.

Before Dr. Keith let me off the exam table, he administered some quick taps and thumps on energy points of my body to stimulate them. He instructed me to stay away from any and all sugars. Even things that would be broken down into sugars like all the carbohydrates I loved to eat. He gave me a list with everything I was to stay away from. Reading it was depressing. It turned out the only thing I could eat were proteins from meats and fish and green vegetables. The only thing I could drink was water and unsweetened tea. This was not going to be easy. He also gave me a couple of antiparasitic supplements to take before eating. No drugs or medications. These were holistic therapies. I liked it!

I didn't think it would be all that hard to follow his instructions but the first week was torture! I was surprised how many foods had sugar in them. I started reading labels on everything. It turns out, if it's processed food, it likely has sugar in it. Manufacturers do that on purpose because sugar is addictive and they want consumers to eat more of their products. It's all about profit, not nutrition or good health. To get my mind off the crazy food cravings I was having, I did a lot of research on the effects of sugar on the body. It affects the brain the same way heroin does. It's also toxic, just like any household poison. It causes sickness in the body. Think about how devastating diabetes is on the human body.

I received that miracle that I was looking for! When the two weeks were over, I had all my vim and vigor back. I once again had the energy of a teenager and my bowels were functioning better than ever. I couldn't wait to see Dr. Keith and thank him for helping me get my life back.

Two weeks later I found myself sitting back on Dr. Keith's table. When he walked into the examination room I was startled. At five feet ten inches and a trim athletic build, he looked like a model from the J. Crew catalogue. I immediately noticed his warm, loving energy when he flashed me his brilliant smile in my direction. I was so sick on my first visit I hadn't noticed any of this. It was no wonder all of his clients ended up crushing on him.

We exchanged pleasantries and he jumped right in doing muscle testing on me again. This time I knew what he was doing. I had spent a lot of time learning about Total Body Modification (TBM). I found the reading fascinating; I highly recommend looking into it. Muscle testing and TBM were forms of Kinesiology. Kinesiology recognizes that the human body has an intelligence separate from the mind often referred to as the "innate." The body knows everything there is to know about itself. Muscle Testing is an easy way to access that information. Dr. Keith reported that all the parasites were under control. He said I could slowly reintroduce sugar back into my diet on a limited basis as long as I continued to take the antiparasitic supplements. After results like these, I was a devout believer and would have done anything he said.

On the way home from Dr. Keith's, I bought a gallon of vanilla ice cream which is my favorite. I served myself a big bowl and proceeded to fulfill my biggest craving from the last two weeks. It tasted unbelievably good! I was in sugar heaven. Halfway into the bowl I started to get a bad headache and my tummy didn't feel all that great either. I was shocked. My body was having a negative reaction to the sugar almost instantaneously. Undeniable proof for me that sugar truly is toxic to the body. I never finished the bowl of ice cream. I ended up giving the rest of the gallon away to a friend. To this day, I try to stay away from processed sugar. It's almost impossible to avoid it all together, but I make the effort. When I do decide to indulge and have a piece of cake or ice cream, I know that for the next hour I'm not going to feel very well. A constant reminder of how toxic sugar really is.

I started seeing Dr. Keith on a regular basis. I learned more about energetic healing. A lot of what he did was harmonizing an individual's vibration to whatever it was that they were having a problem with, such as allergies. Sometimes he would go a different route and ask what happened to me at a certain age. I would instantly know what he was fishing for. He would then have me focus on the experience while he cleared it from my body. I learned that much disease in the body is rooted in experiences we had earlier in life that we didn't process in a healthy way at the time. It gets stored in the body and causes disease later down the road. Dr. Keith would clear the energy, always with a tap, tap and thump, thump, on the appropriate energy center. Sometimes he had to go to a past life to find the root of a problem. The results were always amazing. The issue I was having would clear up immediately or soon after.

I told everybody I knew about the "miracles" Dr. Keith was manifesting. I sent many of my clients to him which wasn't the smartest thing to do. Once Dr. Keith cleared up their issue, they didn't need me anymore. I was happy for them, but it wasn't good for my business. I didn't care. What was important was that people found the healing they were looking for. The first six months I went to Dr Keith I was able to get an appointment with him that day or the day after. After that, he became so busy, I had to wait a week or two to get to see him. Word of mouth is the best form of advertisement. Dr Keith recognized my contribution to his success and honored it by working on me for free for a while. After that, it was always at a reduced rate.

I saw Dr. Keith at his office until I moved out of the state. After I moved, he would work on me remotely, over the phone. When you work on an energetic level, distance and time doesn't exist. It was wonderful to see and experience him evolve over the years. At some point he developed the ability to see the human body in the 4th and 5th dimensions. He could actually see where the energy was blocked and how it needed to be moved. Of course, whoever is being healed has to participate in the healing. He would have me hold a memory or a thought of the root cause of an issue and visualize it moving out of my physicality. Eventually he started talking to entities in the room that only he could see. I never questioned each new level of healing he reached and mastered. I knew that just because I couldn't see or do something did not mean somebody else could not. I blessed Dr. Keith every day when I did my gratitude list.

Years later on a trip back to Cleveland, I saw Dr. Keith in his office. We started reminiscing about how far I had come in my healing. He recalled the first time I sat on his table. I had on crumpled clothes and a bandana on my head covering my greasy hair that I was too sick to wash. I was in pretty bad shape. He confided in me that he never told me how sick I really was. He said it was a good thing I made it to him when I did because if I hadn't, I would have died. I remembered how sick I was, so that bit of information didn't surprise me. It did make me realize how divinely guided I have always been. Universe kept drawing my attention to his ad and I kept ignoring it until I had no choice. I guess at that point of my life I had to be that close to death to be open to the kind of holistic healing Dr. Keith provided. The whole experience opened me up to being an energetic healer by witnessing another one in action. There is nothing like learning from the master first hand.

No longer did the results seem miraculous. Through reading and the actual experience of being energetically healed, I understood that modern medicine as we know it is primitive. All it does is prescribe drugs to manage symptoms without addressing the cause. It also encourages the cutting of the body to remove parts that are there for a reason. Not removing the cause of why they think it needs to be removed in the first place - the root cause. Taking healing to a quantum level finds the root or original cause of disease and enables a healer to clear and remove it for good. Dr. Keith was taking the art of healing to a new, higher level. I accepted and trusted him completely.

I eventually moved across the country to the deserts of the southwest. All my family, friends, and clients were sad to see me leave. I was taken by surprise by how many people went out of their way to express deep gratitude for what I had done for them and how I had changed their lives for the better. They told me stories of how I managed to say just the right thing to help them or change whatever was causing a difficult time in their lives. Some expressed gratitude for empowering them with courage to make big changes that improved their lives. Across the board, people applauded me for living my truth, ignoring social conventions, and creating a life that was unique to bringing myself happiness. Apparently, you can effect powerful change in lives just by being a positive example. Up until then, I had never thought of myself in that way, but so many people went out of their way to thank me as I was getting ready to leave, making it hard to deny the truth. It's important to live your truth and walk your talk not only for yourself, but for those that may be watching.

During the three days it took me to drive across the country I thought about all the accolades I received. Maybe, in my own way, I was more of a healer than I realized. As I was learning, healing takes place on more than a physical or medical level. I knew that massage can powerfully affect the body and mind in positive ways. I facilitated healing in the course of my body work enabling people to move through life with greater stress-free ease. I knew that massage augmented traditional healing and sped up the process. It made me smile when I thought about how being a massage therapist helped fulfill my dream of being a great healer. Maybe, like Dr. Keith, I was taking my healing to new levels without even knowing it. I opened up to the idea that the words which flowed so easily with clients and friends came from a higher vibrational dimension of myself that I was accessing without realizing it.

I ended up in Bisbee, Arizona, a small mountain town in a canyon high up in the Mule Mountains about an hour down the road from historic Tombstone on route 80. It was once a thriving copper mining hub but when the mine closed in the eighties, unemployment skyrocketed. People moved away and left behind a lot of cheap real estate. Old hippies and New Ager's flocked in from California where it was becoming too expensive to live. They created a very special, unique community that embraced the ideals from the sixties: Peace, love, and harmony that dove tailed well with the New Age concept of universal oneness. Alternative living and energetic healing practices had space to thrive. Both factions recognized the planet as their mother that needed to be treated with love and respect. All of these ideals came together and flourished and the town slowly gentrified into a prototype for eco-friendly, alternative living where all its members were treated with empathy and compassion, a utopian microcosm. I fit right in.

The town became a hotbed for alternative healing with a variety of modalities. Not only did they have a few massage therapists, they had Acupuncture, Acupressure, Psychics, Ayurveda, Homeopathy, Naturopathy, Oriental Medicines, Biofeedback, Reiki, Reflexology, and Chiropractic. Impressive for a small town with a low economic impact. The healing community recognized that some people in town could not afford treatments. To remedy that, there was a free clinic offered one Saturday a month where anyone could sign up for two healing sessions of their choice. That's just the kind of community it was. As my massage work began to be known, I was asked to offer my services at the clinic as well.

These clinics took place in the reception hall of an old church. Since it was a temporary set up, they had curtained partitions on wheels to demarcate space and provide a minimal amount of privacy. Being as tall as I am, I was able to see right over them. There was always an older woman, sixtyish, who would set up in the corner in front of a window that I had not met before. She had a white poodle perm and an impish smile. There was something about her energy that continually attracted my attention. I always said that giving a massage was like reading Braille. My fingers could feel trouble spots in the body and respond accordingly. I had done it for so many years, it was almost automatic. While my fingers did the walking, I watched the woman in the corner.

I found out her name was Susan and the healing modality she practiced was called Spiritual Response Therapy, or SRT. I had never heard of it before. People said amazing things about her abilities and her spots on the sign-up sheet always filled up first. As a therapy provider, I was allowed one free session a month with another provider. Five months went by before I found myself sitting at Susan's table in the corner. We exchanged introductions and she welcomed me to town. She proceeded to tell me how she worked. After grounding herself, she connected with her higher self, other entities that were available to work with her that day, and the innate ability of my body to divine information from the spirit realm. I use the word 'divine' on purpose. It turned out what she did was similar to Water Witching with a divining rod, a Y shaped tree branch used for finding underground water, except she used a pendulum and a series of charts to glean information. Both practices fall under the header Dowsing. The definition of Dowsing is observing the motion of a pointer or pendulum that changes in direction in response to unseen influences.

My session with Susan was powerful. Everything she came up with was spot on. Once she uncovered an issue, she would look for the root cause of it. With that, she had enough information to clear it. I know it may sound a little simplistic but why should healing have to be complicated and timely? She warned me that healing was a two-person endeavor. She could clear something, but I had to make the effort not to repeat the old pattern. She guaranteed me that it wouldn't take long for the Universe to test me to see if I learned the associated lesson. I left that day lighter from all the clearing she did and happy knowing that I had found a new tool to continue my never-ending healing process.

Every time I had a friend or family member in town for a visit on one of the Free Healing Clinic Saturdays, I would sign them up for a session with Susan. Everyone would leave with a positive story to tell about how Susan knew something she couldn't have possibly known and found the root cause that always made sense as to why they developed an issue around it. It confirmed to me that Susan was the real deal, not that I needed confirmation. It seemed like wherever I went, I found an amazing healer to work with. I always tried to have a session with her without being too greedy about it.

The more I worked with Susan, the more interested I became in learning the modality she used. I was getting ready to travel for an extended period of time. I traveled enough to know there is always a lot of down time, especially when waiting for various forms of transportation. I always made sure to have a couple good books with me. The next time I saw her I asked if she could recommend reading material on SRT so I could learn more about it. She was obviously pleased by my inquiry. She explained that the first time she worked with me she sensed I had unusually high vibrating energy. So, she took the liberty to ask with her pendulum if I was a good candidate to learn the modality. The pendulum delivered a powerful "yes" response. She laughed and said that she had been patiently waiting for me to ask about it. In response to my question, she asked if I was interested in her becoming my mentor to learn her technique? I didn't even have to think about it. I was absolutely interested in learning energetic healing!

I explained that I was leaving for six months of travel in two weeks. Susan offered to meet with me for three hours every day until I left. I couldn't believe how generous she was offering me her precious time. Not only was she generous with her time, but she gave me my first pendulum, which I still have, several books, and my first set of charts which I have greatly expanded over the years.

It was a natural fit for me from the very beginning. I picked it up quickly and displayed accuracy from the start. I learned that dowsing was a way to access information that is always available from the ever-present innate intelligence of the human body making it an effective tool to uncover issues and their cause and then to clear them. As I learned to trust myself and what came to me, a door would open up in my consciousness, and the answer to a question I was asking was there. I learned that sometimes, when the information didn't present itself, the timing was off. Either I or the person requesting healing wasn't ready to be gifted with it. In essence, I was a conduit for the higher dimensions to communicate with the person I was working with.

Susan was the perfect mentor as she was patient, understanding, and informative. I will always live in gratitude for everything she did for me. One of the interesting things I found out about Susan was her path to becoming a healer. Originally, she was a high-powered lawyer. A friend had asked her to accompany them on a healing retreat. Susan didn't understand what it would be about. She just thought that it would be a nice getaway weekend. It turned out it was a seminar on SRT. Susan went and immediately recognized that this was what she was supposed to be doing with her life. She returned as a changed woman. She quit her job and became an energetic healer full time. Another great example of somebody being divinely guided to their destiny.

In the six months that I was gone, I perfected my skill and built confidence when swinging the pendulum. I had many wonderful experiences working with the people I met along the way. One night in particular stands out that I would like to share. I was on Taveuni Island in Fiji looking at potential real estate. For the most part, the island remained untouched by the outside world. I became friendly with a woman named Mary who ran the campground I was staying at. I explained that I was learning about energetic healing and that I was looking for people to practice on. She was instantly intrigued, took my hand, and guided me to some shade under a nearby tree where I worked with her for the next hour. I must have hit a home run, because she invited me to come to her village that night and meet some of her family and friends. I spent the evening sitting on her front porch surrounded by what seemed like half the village. I took turns working on the curious group coming up with some surprising and significant healing with Mary acting as translator when needed because I knew very little Fijian. As word of my ability spread, more and more people started showing up. I was kept busy well into the night. The whole evening seemed surreal to me. There I was, in the middle of nowhere, having a magical moment with these wonderfully open souls. I was starting to feel like an authentic energetic healer. It felt very right to me.

When I returned, Susan continued to meet with me. Instead of every day, we met once a month for an afternoon. She was pleased with my progress and the confidence I was developing in my work. As I advanced, she would expand on what the pendulum and energetic healing could actually do. I was doubly amazed when she showed me how I could do chiropractic adjustments. I swear, when she demonstrated it on me, I could actually feel the adjustment happening inside my body! Over the years, every time I do an adjustment on a client, I get that same response from them.

To this day, I continue to expand my knowledge by reading about other dowsing therapists and how they work. I keep adding more charts and modalities to what I use. I have incorporated many systems and created some of my own which have cultivated into my own unique practice. There seems no end to what can be accomplished with energetic restructuring, as I have come to call it. As long as a person is open and willing to do the associated work.

In the beginning, I was constantly looking for people to practice on. Unfortunately, it was a little bit too 'out there' for most people and they would decline a free session. I felt very lucky when a friend was open to it. One of those friends was Pauline. I met her soon after I arrived in Bisbee. It was one of those synchronistic moments when the Universe worked to bring two old souls together. She had grown up on a ranch outside of town and lived there most of her life so she already knew I was recent arrival. She just came over to me, introduced herself, and welcomed me to Bisbee. It didn't take her long before she started filling me in on the do's and don'ts around town. Her life experiences were very different from mine growing up on a ranch in the desert. She was a great storyteller and I loved to listen to her wild west adventures.

We were drawn to each other like magnets. It was one of those friendships that happened as soon as our eyes met, like we had known each other forever. I always had a strong sense that we spent some past lives together in Egypt. I considered her my spiritual soul sister. We even resembled each other in body type, hair, and our steely blue eyes that held the wisdom of the ages. Pauline was just beginning her exploration down the spiritual road. Lucky for her, spirituality was my favorite topic to talk about and I quickly got her from a walk to a run. Every time we got together, we couldn't share fast enough the latest book we read, program we watched, or experience we had that offered some new epiphany about our spiritual experience and evolution on the planet.

Pauline was interested in my new healing endeavor and readily agreed to let me work on her. I set up in her living room, checked in with our higher selves and spirit guides, and off we went.

When we were done, she was excited about what had happened, thanked me, and shared how I hit upon some important issues in her life. She easily accepted everything that had just happened as part of her new reality.

After the session Pauline became noticeably quiet. It was obvious that she was struggling with something as she nervously played with her hands. I sat patiently and sent her love and support while I waited for her to share. Finally, she started to tell me about her son Kennedy who lived a three-hour drive to the north. It turned out he had been struggling with advanced alcoholism for years and was now getting to the point that the damage he was doing to his liver would be irreversible. Unfortunately, he didn't seem to have the motivation or desire to make changes even though he was aware that he was killing himself. Pauline had tried everything she could think of to rescue her son from himself. She eventually realized that she was powerless until Kennedy decided he wanted to make changes. That didn't stop Pauline. As she learned new things in the realm of alternative healing, she would covertly try them on Kennedy without him knowing, but so far didn't have any success. One of her attempts that I found fascinating was energizing his alcohol with an amethyst crystal. It was supposed to make the alcohol distasteful so he wouldn't want to drink it. It didn't stop Kennedy. She knew he would never be open to the kind of healing work I was doing but asked if I could do something anyways. I knew from working with Dr. Keith, that when it came to energetic healing, it could be done remotely so the distance wouldn't be an issue. I had worked on many people remotely when I was traveling so, I agreed to do work on

Kennedy and see where it went. What was the worst that could happen?

The first thing I did was connect with Kennedy and his higher self. I immediately asked his higher self if I had permission to work on him. I was relieved when I received a positive response with the pendulum. I then cleared his energies of anything that would prevent me from receiving 100% accuracy like personal judgments, assumptions, beliefs, programs, and fears, following my usual protocol. It's important to have permission. I have no right to foist something on a person and interfere with their life plan if they don't want it. I proceeded to go through the charts with one topic leading to another. I came up with some root causes why he drank and did my best to clear them out. I then worked on why he was resistant to becoming sober, found some reasons that seemed to make sense and cleared those as well. Pauline kept nodding her head in agreement with everything that came up. The pendulum let me know when it was time to end the session. As with all my clients, I blessed him with the wisdom and tools to heal and move forward on his path.

Pauline and I sat there speechless. She was definitely having a moment. It is hard to love somebody and watch them destroy their lives and be powerless to do anything about it. Eventually, she thanked me for doing what I could. She also shared with me that through the session with Kennedy, she had a better understanding of where he was at and why he was doing what he was. I was grateful to have the ability to alleviate some of her suffering. I knew she needed to be alone so I packed up my valise and left her to her thoughts.

A few weeks later I received a call from Pauline. She was excited to tell me that Kennedy had joined Alcoholics Anonymous! She was totally incredulous at this new turn of events and said my healing work must have had an effect on him. She was chomping at the bit to tell me the story of how it came about. Apparently, as the story goes, a few random church ladies showed up at Kennedy's door with food one afternoon. They were reaching out to the community providing food to those who needed it. The timing could not have been better. The ladies asked Kennedy if he was hungry and as fate would have it, he was. He invited the women in and accepted their offerings. He liked the them and listened politely to the information they were sharing while he ate. They told him about their church and the community it served. Kennedy wasn't religious, but for some unexplainable reason agreed to accompany the women to their church and meet the people there. Kennedy didn't have any friends and was lonely. At the church, he enjoyed having people around him that embraced and affirmed him. He met many sincere people that opened up their arms to him. Some of them were in Alcoholics Anonymous and when Kennedy told them his story, they invited him to attend a meeting. He must have liked the group because he kept going back.

We live in a dynamic, energetic world that is multilayered with its own intelligence. I think it is so intricate that our primitive minds can't comprehend how it all fits together. There are many energies at play at any given moment which create infinite possibilities. One thing leads to another and something is provided just when the person is ready. What we ultimately choose to do depends on our free will. Was this turn of events already mapped out in the blueprint of Kennedy's life? Was it just a coincidence that it happened soon after I did the energy work on him? Did I facilitate this new development with him through my dowsing work? The joy I felt for Pauline and for Kennedy was powerful. It was wonderful to hear the relief in her voice. I didn't say anything about the session we did on him. It didn't matter why he was suddenly in the right place to make a positive choice; it was just important that he did.

I sat there for quite some time with my thoughts running wild. What Pauline told me was miraculous! I was happy to be of service, especially to somebody I cared so much about. I started thinking about all the people I had helped along the way and the people who helped me. Massage clients that graced my table depending on me to stroke away all their pain and stress. Many others that shared their problems with me and how I had somehow managed to say just the right thing to help them through. When I needed to heal, I attracted wonderfully gifted healers to make my physical experience easier and pain free. I marveled at how the Universe brought me teachers when I was ready to open up to higher levels of understanding and wisdom. Betty, my yoga guru, taught me about balance between the body, mind, and spirit. Dr. Keith opened me up to healing on a quantum, multidimensional level. And now Susan gifted me with a modality to access and direct my own inner healer. The more I became comfortable and trusting of the information I received while working with someone, I realized this is what I had been doing all along. I was a Medical Intuitive! I just didn't know I was doing it.

Many people on evolutionary healing paths were doing the same thing I was doing but in their own way. No two healers work in quite the same way. We were learning to step out of the third dimension and work in higher dimensions. When we recognize the interconnectedness of the Universe on a vibrational level, we can effect positive change using the simple laws of physics. We often feel or become intuitively aware of the connections being made between the physical and the higher vibrational dimensions. I often use the example of an old-fashioned telephone switchboard operator using a giant universal switch board. The parallel between plugging cords on the switchboard is similar to the connections being made between people, souls, dimensions, guides, and other entities. All the healer needs to know is what connections to make.

Yes, humans are not alone in the universe. There is infinite help out there in the ethers. We only need to open up and ask for it.

My mind suddenly opened up to that sunny afternoon when the younger version of myself was walking on the beach dreaming of being a healer. I realized what I was doing that afternoon was setting my intention to be divinely gifted. Over the years, I watched with a little bit of envy when healers performed what I jokingly called their Voodoo Magic. I strongly desired to be of service just like them. I realized that young man's intention had now become my reality. With every new healing experience, with each new teacher that lovingly shared their skills and knowledge with me, and every client that put their faith and trust in me, my own potential to be a healer expanded. Now, with the transition in full swing, the planet is receiving higher vibrational energies that are revealing new healing technologies using quantum physics, magnetics, and knowledge that everything is a frequency that can be positively affected. The veil is growing thinner making it easier to remember all the wisdom of the ages and communicate in a multi-dimensional universe where highly evolved beings are waiting to assist in our advancement. Time, learning, and evolution are moving much quicker now giving me the opportunity to be more than I ever imagined. We are powerful creative beings manifesting our realities moment by moment. Everything we think is a vibration that becomes an intention that we attract towards us. We must always be mindful of our thoughts. Keep them marinating in positivity so we can manifest our dreams come true. My aspiration of being an energetic healer is becoming a reality for me in this lifetime. I know that I'm still at the beginning of my path to mastery. I imagine miraculous instantaneous healing in our futures!

DREAM IT!

Mr. Hollywood

I spent eighteen years learning as much as I could about spirituality and how it manifests in the human experience. I got in touch with my pain and anger and practiced releasing it daily. With the help of various healers, I addressed why I attracted certain experiences both physically and emotionally and cleared all the blocks, beliefs, imprints, vows, contracts, past experiences, genetics, and negative past life energies that I found. I had reached a plateau where life worked with me and for me, helping me manifest all I desired. I understood I was responsible for everything. Most importantly, I understood that happiness was not contingent on somebody else making me happy, but instead came from within and then was to be shared with those around me. I was happy with my independence. I felt self-actualized.

I was at a dinner party in my early forties where I was the only one at the table that was not in a relationship. One of the guests asked me why that was? I explained that I was only fifty percent of the relationship equation. All I could do was continually work to be the best version of myself so when the other fifty percent showed up, I would have something exceptional to share with them. I knew enough to know that relationships don't work if you go into them for the wrong reasons. To commit to a relationship for self-serving reasons or for the sake of being in a relationship was asking for trouble.

The Universe conspired a few years later to finally gift me a relationship and give me an opportunity to put everything I thought that I had learned into practice. It happened the first week of January 2005 and it changed my life forever.

Mr. Hollywood, a new massage client who was coming to town on business for only one night, booked a massage with me three days in advance. I showed up for the appointment at the allotted time and knocked on his hotel room door. When he opened it, I was instantly unnerved. I recognized something in him immediately. I played it cool and was professional. While he was getting on the massage table, I excused myself and went into the bathroom where I proceeded to go into a panic. There was something about him that totally threw me off. I wondered If I could even provide him a good massage. I set my resolve, went out, and sadly, gave him one of the worst massages I ever did. Afterward, we started talking as I was getting my equipment ready to leave. We ended up talking for a couple of hours with me standing at the door with my massage table in one hand and my equipment bag in the other. There was obviously an attraction here given the covert flirting that was passing between us. I wanted to know what was going on, so I reverted to astrology. Before I left, I asked him for his birth information so I could do his chart. Surprisingly, he even knew what time he was born. I rushed home to do his chart. In my craziness, I ended up with the wrong rising sign. He was born in Grasse which explained the French accent. Grasse is Central European Time and all of my astrology books were in Eastern Standard Time. I must have done the math wrong converting his birth time in France to Eastern Standard Time in the United States. If I had done his chart correctly the night we met, I never would've considered a relationship with him.

That wasn't the only event that happened that makes me believe the Universe conspired to get us together. A month passed before I saw Mr. Hollywood again. He was a salesman for a pharmaceutical company and he traveled a lot for work. The fact that we lived on opposite sides of the country didn't help either. We got to know each other that first month over nightly marathon phone calls. I liked hearing his French accent say the most wonderful things to me. I fell in love with him over the phone. Not the best way to fall in love I later discovered. At the end of the fourth week, Mr. Hollywood was complaining one night that his assistant couldn't get him on a flight home until Saturday night. He was unhappy he had a night in Washington, D.C. with nothing to do. I jokingly informed him that D.C. was only a five-hour drive for me. I instantly fantasized making the drive for a night to finally consummate the relationship. He thought that was a brilliant idea but instead of driving, he suggested I fly down for the night. I'm typically not the kind of person to do extravagant things at the last minute but for some reason I thought, "Why not?" I told him I would call him back in ten minutes. I hung up and called the airline that had a hub in Cleveland. I told the customer service representative what I wanted to do. I listened while she tapped away on her keyboard. She got back on the line and told me a next day overnight return flight would be $689. I laughed and told her that this wasn't going to happen unless it was under $200, thinking she would tell me tough luck. Instead, she hesitated, then asked me if I would hold the line. I could hear the keys to her keyboard typing away. She returned to the line and happily informed me she could get me to D.C. and back for $169. I bought the ticket. The next night was one for the history books! I never slept.

I tried doing that several times again over the years and it never worked a second time. Why did it work that time? There is no doubt in my mind that my relationship with Mr. Hollywood was my destiny and there were unknown energies conspiring to make sure it happened.

The attraction between us was off the charts. We were like two magnets that couldn't be kept apart. Our physical bodies were exactly what the other fantasied about. Mr. Hollywood was an inch shorter than me with a thick, stocky build that drove me crazy. His square face featured mystical green eyes that always suggested mischievous thoughts and a mop of dirty blonde curls that added to the allure of playfulness. And the accent... how could I resist!

Four months later, when I found out I had calculated Mr. Hollywood's Rising Sign wrong, it was too late. I was already madly in love. I chose to ignore the fact that his actual Rising Sign was not a good fit for me. Not only was it not a good fit, but the negative side of it predicted he would be a manipulative and unfaithful liar. That was the first sign I ended up choosing to ignore along the way. There were more waiting right around the corner.

The relationship developed quickly. It was right out of a Hollywood movie rendezvousing in one city after another at least once a month. Through his work travels, he had accrued a lot of frequent flier miles that he used to fly me for weekends wherever he found himself. In the first year, I went to Seattle, San Francisco, New York, Phoenix, D.C. a second time, Tampa, and the Grand Canyon. The latter is where he proposed marriage at the bottom of the canyon on the foot bridge spanning the Colorado River. He was always the perfect Prince Charming, treating me like a King. Being a Leo, that felt great. His favorite city was Los Angeles and he knew people in the entertainment industry so we would stay at their guest houses in Beverly Hills. That is when I started referring to him as Mr. Hollywood. Who wouldn't be blinded by that.

We talked about making the relationship permanent but my intuition held me back. I kept feeling that he wasn't ready for the life I dreamt of. For some reason, monogamy has always been important to me. I felt if we weren't exclusive, the relationship would amount to nothing more than friends with benefits. We talked about it extensively. He was adamant that he was ready for, and wanted a monogamous relationship. I couldn't shake the feeling he still needed time to sow some wild oats. There were other things he said that also didn't feel true to me. In the past, I had been suspicious of people who agreed with everything that I said. Being the consummate salesman, Mr. Hollywood was very good at saying what he thought I wanted to hear. If I had it for a goal, suddenly it was his goal too. Once again, I ignored what my intuition was telling me and bought what Mr. Hollywood was selling.

Christmas of 2005 found us on a private island in Tahiti. It had to be the most romantic experience that had ever happened to me. I couldn't believe somebody like me from a small city and a meager upbringing was living the life I now found myself in. The place was practically empty because of the holiday. We decided we were going to walk around the whole island via the beach. We found ourselves on the other side of the island which was deserted, swimming naked in the warm water, with the mountains of Bora Bora looming on a distant island. I was lying on top of him in about six inches of water. I looked down at his face and noticed schools of mini black and white fish swimming around his head. I was overcome by the moment. I thought to myself, if I were ever to propose marriage, this was the perfect moment. Even though I said no to his proposal in the Grand Canyon months earlier, I decided to take a chance and ask him now. I ignored all my reservations and concerns and asked Mr. Hollywood to marry me. He enthusiastically said, "Yes!" We rolled around in total bliss scaring all the fish away. When we settled down, they returned. We jokingly named them *wedding fish*.

It was official. I was going to sell my house and live with him in Bisbee, Arizona. After the holidays, I put my beautiful old baronial house that I was actively restoring up for sale. I started making plans to move out west to live with Mr. Hollywood in the desert. All my friends and family were incredulous that I would give up my career, a clientele that took me years to build, lifelong friends, and my family to be with this guy. I explained that the moment was defining who I was. Was I a man who lived for material gain or somebody who lived in the moment and took a chance on love? Secretly, I thought at my age it may be my last chance. I was 45 years old. I knew my network of friends and family were concerned about my well-being and wanted me to be happy. I loved them dearly for caring. But once my mind is made up, I rarely change it.

It took eight months for my house to sell. We were in our second year and Mr. Hollywood's facade was beginning to crack. I would often say that you really don't know somebody until after a year. The first year everybody is on their best behavior. During the second year, people start getting lazy and their true colors start popping out. We continued to travel while we waited for the house to sell. We went to South America for a month in June. It was the longest we had been together at one time. As I write this, I suddenly think about how crazy I was basing a life altering decision of marriage on a slew of romantic weekends. Two different things happened on the South American trip that, in retrospect, defined the following six years.

First, I corrected Mr. Hollywood in front of the manager of the exclusive Explora Lodge in Patagonia, Chile. He was trying to impress the manager upon our arrival, and told a blatant lie about me. He ignored what I said and continued to get us checked in. The entire time he had a big smile on his face, but I could feel his sudden angry and negative energy. I knew he was not happy about what I had said. Once our bags were in the room, he left and I didn't see him for the following two days. He literally disappeared and left me alone in the wilderness of Patagonia. When he showed up two days later, he never mentioned anything about his disappearance, and I never asked.

The second thing happened soon after, in Calafate, Argentina, where I wanted to go and see the calving glaciers. Mr. Hollywood was unhappy with the accommodations. The only place to stay in town was a hostel that had rooms with a shared bath. That was not on par to his typical standard of luxury, so he decided we weren't going to stay there. He had toyed with the idea of going to Ushuaia, Chile, the southernmost city in the world, but it wasn't on our itinerary. Suddenly, that was his new must-do destination that couldn't be missed. We went to a travel agent. I stayed outside on the side walk taking in the funky town while he went in to see what the options were. He came out and informed me that we could get on a plane to Ushuaia that evening even though all the flights out of Ushuaia were booked already, or we could go to Buenos Aires early and have an extra week there. I instantly voted for an extra week in Buenos Aires. He gave me a dismayed look and without a word went back into the travel agent and booked two tickets for Ushuaia. Getting out of Ushuaia ended up being a lengthy nightmare, shortening our stay in Buenos Aires considerably.

I don't know why I chose to ignore his unacceptable behavior, but I did. I couldn't reconcile my brain around it. His actions were totally incongruent with the man he made himself out to be. Maybe I tricked myself into believing they were isolated events brought on by the stress of traveling. I stayed true to my commitment to move and make the relationship work.

The house finally sold in August. I packed up what was left of my worldly possessions in preparation for moving day. I was surprised by how many friends and neighbors showed up to help load everything up. It turned into one big love fest. Mr. Hollywood was acting strangely. Instead of his usual charming and charismatic self, he was quiet and distant. I think the reality of seeing my household belongings being loaded onto a truck suddenly made my move real to him. During the day, I was too preoccupied to give it much thought. When we finally got into the truck to start our three-day drive across the country, I noticed his mood had turned sullen. Before we even drove out of the county, I had a sinking feeling in my stomach that I had just made the biggest mistake of my life. The thought of turning around and staying seemed impossible. I had passed on all of my clients to other massage therapists, and I no longer had a house to live in. There was no going back. I sat looking at the disappearing highway and resolved myself to make the best of things. I still believed I was going to spend the rest of my life with this man, and I had to buck up and make the most of it.

Mr. Hollywood had a meltdown as I was unpacking, putting things away, moving furniture, and hanging pictures. He didn't like the invasion into his space. He wanted to keep things as they were. He obviously didn't think the move through. He had absolutely no empathy or compassion for the fact that I had given up my home and was trying to make a new one for us that reflected both of our personalities. It was suddenly all about him and what he wanted. As he laid in bed and pouted, I continued to unpack my belongings and find new homes for them. I didn't know what else to do. I knew then that we had some work to do in order to move our relationship forward to the phase of cohabitation. I hoped Mr. Hollywood was up to it. Instead, he dealt with the situation by being away on business as much as possible. I didn't mind, I was used to living alone. Sometimes when he was home it seemed like we were getting our magic back. He would be Prince Charming again, all attentive and loving. Especially when there were other people around. I loved those moments, but they never lasted long. It would only be a short time before he would be back on the road again.

While he was gone, I tried to make the most of my new home. Gardening always made me happy, so I proceeded to transform the outdoor spaces into a luscious green, flowered oasis in the middle of the desert. Not an easy task compared to back east where it rained all the time. I settled into the rhythm of the town. It was small with only a couple thousand people. It took me a while, but I think I managed to meet just about everybody. I easily made new friends. I found I had a lot in common with them. I learned about living in a community where people reached out to one another to offer a helping hand. I also thought it was wonderful the way people would get together to celebrate life. There always seemed to be a party or an event going on. I had learned long ago that happiness comes from the inside and it was my responsibility to generate it. I found happiness in Bisbee and with myself.

I began to notice a lot of things now that we were together more. Mr. Hollywood was a storyteller. I would listen to him tell the same story over and over again when different people were visiting. I was shocked to notice that he never told a story the same way twice. He would make things up to fit the audience he was telling it to. He just made it up as he went along. Later, in private, I would point this out which would infuriate him.

Two years into our cohabitation, I discovered Mr. Hollywood was cheating on me. He had left his computer home for an extended trip because the country he was going to was noted for stealing electronics. I was having trouble on my computer, so I decided to use his. When I opened it, there was the complete history on the toolbar of what he was doing the last time he had used it (which was on a short business trip right before he left for the extended one). I was shocked! He had used an escort service and had taken a cash withdrawal for the exact amount needed on the same day. When he traveled, he never used cash. He charged everything because he needed records for his taxes. When I picked him up at the airport, I confronted him in the parking lot. He denied everything. I wouldn't argue until we got home so I could provide the evidence. When I showed him, he still denied everything. He tried to say he had just gotten a massage. Awfully expensive massage! Then he tried to turn the tables on me. How dare I not trust him? How dare I doubt his word? I didn't believe any of it. The next day after he still hadn't fessed up, I closed the door on it. I explained to him if I was wrong, he had to forgive me for believing he had cheated. And, if I was right, I had to live in forgiveness for him. After that, every time I opened his computer, the history was wiped clean. Made me wonder what he was hiding. From that point on, I just assumed he was getting his needs met whenever he went away on business. So much for his desire to be in a monogamous relationship. A part of me felt vindicated that my intuition was right from the very beginning. He never intended to be monogamous

The attention always had to be on him. When I had dinner parties in his absence there would always be a dynamic exchange of ideas with everybody present contributing to conversation. They were a lot of fun and I always looked forward to the diverse company and the stimulating discourse. When he was home, it was a much different experience. The guests had no choice but to sit in silence while he shared his latest traveling adventure, never giving others a chance to speak. After one such evening, I explained how different it was when he was away. He blatantly said he didn't care. He justified himself by saying he had to do the talking or nobody else would. He dismissed me by walking away. We never discussed it again.

Mr. Hollywood was very conscious of public impressions and the opinions of others regarding him. When we entertained or went to public functions, he presented us as the picture-perfect couple. He was attentive and devoted, always holding my hand or throwing his arm around my shoulder. We were the couple everybody wanted to be like. When we would get home, it was a much different scenario. It was like I didn't exist. He would go up to the hot tub by himself and spend hours there. When he was in the house, he usually stayed in the guest room or in his office. It was like living with Dr. Jekyll and Mr. Hyde. His constant metamorphosis made my head spin. It got to the point that I went out of my way to get invited out so I could be with Dr. Jekyll.

The relationship did have its benefits. We were a handsome couple and people treated us well. I never really understood why he was attracted to me, a nobody from nowhere. I liked being defined as his partner. Mr. Hollywood was this worldly, fashionable, jet setter that easily charmed everyone and I got to be all those things too by association. He made good money and we lived nicely. We were always traveling somewhere. Because of him, I got to see the world in a luxurious way. When he was in Prince Charming mode, he made me feel like I was the most important person in the world to be catered to and fawned over.

Towards the end of the relationship, I decided I was going to write a book. My topic: How people allow themselves to be victimized in relationships. I could never understand why people stayed in abusive relationships or left one just to find another and repeat the whole experience with somebody else. I spent months doing research, compiling information, and talking to people. Never once did I clue into my reality, which was that I was being the quintessential victim in my own abusive relationship. I never wrote the book. In retrospect, I can see how my intuitive self was seeding my consciousness with the book idea in order to wake me up to the life I was leading. And, the reality that I was choosing to stay in a very negative situation. It didn't work. When I think back on it, I shake my head in irony. How blind I was to what I was letting happen to me.

As the years slipped by, Mr. Hollywood became increasingly verbally abusive. It would shock me when some mean-spirited, vial comment emerged from him seemingly out of nowhere. I was brought up in a home with parents who couldn't stand one another. For whatever reason they individually tolerated each other for fifty years. There was always a lot of fighting and arguing. I refused to be a couple like my parents were. Instead of arguing with him, I would just walk away in stunned silence. Sometimes I felt like he was goading me on, being more and more hurtful to see what my reaction would be. My intuition told me that he was constantly cheating on me while on his business trips. Why would anybody be faithful to someone they didn't even like? In the last year we were together, it became obvious to me that he wanted out of the relationship. He wouldn't end it himself because he didn't want to be the "bad" guy. What would people think of him? I believe he was pushing me hard to end it by making my life miserable. He needed me to be the bad guy. Unfortunately for him, I had no desire to do that. I had many reasons for staying in the relationship. Top of the list was the small fact that I was still very much in love with him. I couldn't believe that despite all the healing I had done before I met him and the care, I always took to be the best that I could be, I had still attracted a relationship like this.

In the end he got his wish.

On Christmas night, 2011, with a houseful of people, our relationship imploded. I'm embarrassed to say things got physical. Mr. Hollywood was treating me badly in front of our friends. It was the first time that had happened. I wasn't going to tolerate our dirty laundry being aired in front of our friends. While alone in the living room I warned him that if he couldn't treat me nicely in front of our friends, I was going to send everybody home. Without saying a word, he poked me so hard on my chest that I stumbled backwards. It left a bruise which I had for days. I lost it! He had never touched me in anger before. I instinctively pushed him into a corner and balled my hand into a fist to punch him in the head, but something came over me. I hesitated. A voice in my head asked me if I really wanted to be "that person?" Instead of punching him, I brought my leg up quickly and my knee made painful contact with his crotch. As he slid to the floor, I went into the kitchen where our guests were getting dinner ready to address the situation. They didn't need much explanation after the show we had just put on. They gathered their stuff and walked out into the night wishing us luck as they left.

I watched as the last of our guests turned the corner at the bottom of the hill. I went back into the house and joined Mr.

Hollywood in the living room. As soon as I sat down, he released a torrent of angry, hateful accusations detailing how useless and hypocritical he thought I was and that he couldn't stand the sight of me anymore. I was shocked by how much hatred he had for me! His ranting went on for close to thirty minutes, at times not even making sense. I calmly sat there wondering how he managed to live with me for six years when he obviously held nothing but contempt for me. He eventually ran out of steam and sat glaring at me. For the first time, I didn't see the point in fighting for the relationship anymore. I got up and said, "Well that's that" and walked out of the room. The relationship was mercifully over.

I was shell shocked to say the least. Not that it wasn't a long time coming, but now that it happened it seemed so sudden. I was totally unprepared to be single again. I had no backup plan. I truly thought we would be together until one of us passed. I didn't know what to do or where to go. I *did* know I was not going to cohabitate in the same home together. After everything he said I could barely look at him. We needed to sell our home. I had invested all my money in the house to pay it off so we wouldn't have a mortgage payment every month. At the time, I thought it would be a good investment. Now I found myself cash poor. I was consumed by anger and had to force myself to be civil toward him. On the upside, I was excited to get out of the desert. It was never a good fit for me. I needed to be by water.

I had to wait yet again for a house to sell before I would have cash. Without any money, my options were minimal. I ended up crashing with my mother, back in Cleveland, until I could get my feet back on the ground. She was in her late eighties at this point and was happy to have somebody around to help her out. I started seeing Dr. Keith again to help me move through my anger and pain from the separation. Healing from the past seven years was my top priority. Dr. Keith was good enough to offer me a job as a massage therapist at his clinic so I would have some cash flow. Slowly, I reconnected with friends and started getting invites to go out. I have to say, everybody made an effort to keep me busy and distracted. I started feeling like my old self again.

A friend of mine from Bisbee decided to look at my astrological natal chart to help explain what was going on in my life. She called and told me I had three Pluto transits that hit my chart right before Christmas. Usually, a person has one Pluto transit in a lifetime. She said it was unheard of to have three happening simultaneously. Pluto is the sign of death and rebirth. Its influence is intense, life altering and profound, forcing us to explore the truths that lie beneath the surface and morph them into something new. I researched them in detail on the computer. The energy from the transits were playing out in the worst possible way. It helped to know what I was working with. Pluto transits last for two years. I had no choice but to do my best to get through it. The description for each transit ended with: Life would be totally different than when the transit began. I was curious as to where I would be in two years.

Six months passed and I was slowly coming out of my shock. Suddenly, I needed some answers. I emailed Mr. Hollywood with some questions and concerns. I had not allowed any communication with him since the day I moved out. He replied to my email immediately. I didn't like what it had to say. Not surprisingly, it was apparent had been lying and cheating on me from the very beginning. The biggest lie, the one that I based my decision to move on, was his desire to be in a monogamous relationship. The man didn't even *believe* in monogamy. He confessed that he simply told me what I wanted to hear to convince to move in with him. He explained that he figured after a couple of years I would change my mind and we would be free to have sex with whomever. That lie took me the longest to get over. Then he callously bragged about all the sex he was now having without any consideration how that information would make me feel. Instead of helping me, these discoveries only fueled my hurt and anger. I decided end communication with him, except to get the house sold.

Since I didn't have Mr. Hollywood to talk with, I talked to everybody else. I spared no one my sad story about how I partnered with the devil and all the bad things he had perpetrated against me. It was a good way to release my rage but I'm sure I bored the hell out of everyone who dared to ask how I was doing. I must have sounded pretty pathetic. I can't believe my friends tolerated me so lovingly the way they all did.

I met a fellow massage therapist at Dr. Keith's clinic. Not only did she give a fantastic massage, but she incorporated her ability to read the body and convey what was stored in trouble areas before releasing it. She was extremely talented at what she did. Her name was Jane. She had thick blonde hair and brownish green cat eyes that were mesmerizing. Needless to say, her positive energy was off the charts. We were destined to be good friends.

Jane loved hearing my "Mr. Hollywood" stories. It turned out she was divorced from her own devil incarnate. She was the one who blessed me with the name for what I was dealing with: A narcissist. It was almost creepy how similar our stories were. We spent hours together talking about it. I did my research and was not surprised that Mr. Hollywood was a textbook narcissist. I'm going to add sociopathic as well because he left the lives of all the people he had ever been in a relationship with in total carnage. He knew what he was doing but he didn't care as long as he got what he wanted at the moment. Having the term - narcissist - validated my experience and the characteristics helped me to understand how I had been manipulated so easily. It also helped to know that I wasn't the only one that had fallen for the charms and lies of narcissists.

It was wonderful to finally have somebody I felt really understood what I had gone through. The entire time I was with Mr. Hollywood, I never shared what my private life was like with anyone. Outwardly, I was living the romantic fantasy come true. Prince Charming and his King living in an exotic location and traveling the world. On one of her many visits to Bisbee, my niece, Lindsey, said to me that my relationship with Mr. Hollywood was the only healthy one she had witnessed. Other people had expressed the same sentiment. There was a lot of outside pressure to not dispel the illusion. A part of me wanted it to be true. The other factor that played into my silence was that I was confused for years by the incongruency of what Mr. Hollywood said versus what he actually did. It never made sense. Honestly, I was embarrassed by it all. I was the classic victim, sorry to say.

I recognized that Mr. Hollywood and his sociopathic narcissism wasn't the problem. The problem was me! Why did I attract someone like him in the first place and why did I put up with his abusive behavior for so long? Where did my victim mentality come from? I had never put up with anybody treating me badly in the past. Three strikes and you're out was my motto. Bring on to the next one. I had to ask myself some tough questions. But before I could do that, I needed to get past my ego which kept me in a place of rage and making Mr. Hollywood responsible for my misery. As always, when the student is ready the teacher appears.

A friend of mine must have recognized that I was stuck and needed some help. They gifted me with a copy of the Eckhart Tolle book, *A New Earth*. It was worn and tattered and had obviously been read quite a few times. The patina made it all that more intriguing. I started reading it one night and didn't put it down for the next month. I had to read it over and over to make sure I understood what I was reading. I realized my ego had taken over the best of me and I needed to let it go. I had read about the ego before and thought I did a good job of managing it, but this book put everything into an entirely different light. Before I demonize the ego, let me clarify that it plays an important function of protecting us from acting on our basic urges and perceiving threats to our safety in the external world. It controls our consciousness and helps integrate the outer world with our inner world. But, oftentimes, it inflates feelings of pride and superiority over others, thus clouding our perceptions.

Ego takes things personally. I blamed everything on Mr. Hollywood, making him the villain in my life. Of course, that made me the victim, suffering because of all his misdeeds. I wallowed in my anger allowing it to fuel my need for him to verbally admit all the wrongs he had done to me. I wanted him to see what had happened, the way I viewed it. I became obsessed with the fantasy of confronting him in person so I could feel superior. I knew I was right and wanted him to admit that he was wrong. I even indulged myself in a fantasy of beating the shit out of him which is a primitive way the ego asserts itself. That particular fantasy always made me feel better in the moment, but ultimately, embarrassed that I could even think of a thing like that. That wasn't who I was. What happened to that loving, forgiving, spiritual being I always thought I was? I was so attached to my story that I became like a dog chewing on a bone spewing my fault finding and complaining to anybody who would listen. In reading the Eckart Tolle book, I realized a part of me didn't want to let go of the relationship. In some twisted way, my pain and suffering kept the relationship alive.

I read the book multiple times until I could almost recite it, yet I couldn't let go of my ego. I was beginning to feel trapped in my negativity. The more I tried to fight off the ego the more I energized it. It's awful to be aware that what you are doing is self-destructive and yet being compelled to keep on doing it. My victimhood became my reason for living. The turning point finally came with an appointment with Dr. Keith. I can only imagine how tired he and everybody else were of listening to my angry blame game. He looked me in the eye and said Mr. Hollywood was never going to give me what I thought I needed. He pointed out that as far as Mr. Hollywood was concerned, he had done nothing wrong. He had already rewritten his story to suit himself. He also reminded me that Mr. Hollywood had moved on and was already in another relationship. I'd given Dr. Keith such authority in my life that hearing those words come out of his mouth was like a slap in the face. I went home and opened the Eckhart Tolle book again and started rereading it yet again.

Finally, thanks to Dr. Keith, I was in a place to let my ego's needs go and become aware and practice being neutral. I learned to detach from my emotions and the outcomes that I thought I wanted and needed, I was able to change my perspective to a third person viewpoint of myself and what I was doing. Every time I caught myself falling back into the past, and outcomes that I had no power over, I pulled myself into the present moment, letting the past go. My new perspective changed everything. I found myself in a place where I could answer those hard questions, I had been asking myself.

I knew that I created my reality, so I had no choice but to take full responsibility for what happened to me. Not an easy thing to do when you are raging with unsettled anger. Acknowledging and accepting this took a few years but eventually I was able to let go. When I did, it got me out of the victim mode so I could see the experience from a more neutral perspective. I started reading and talking to Jane about what kinds of people are attracted to narcissists and what the characteristics are that they seem to have in common. Of those, which ones did I possess? I started to entertain various ideas as to why I would create this experience. How was this serving me? For years it was the main topic I talked about with anyone who would listen. I kept thinking we are here to learn lessons. Okay, what would the lesson be? What was Mr. Hollywood's role in my life? If everything happens for a reason, what did I have to gain from it?

The answers to most of these questions were surprising in their simplicity even though it took me the next five years to figure it all out. The effort was priceless! The lesson I learned changed my entire belief about myself.

Narcissists prey on people who are loving, kind, empathetic, and forgiving. People who look at life from a positive point of view. These are all characteristics that enable a narcissist and give them power. A narcissist initially presents themselves as too good to be true, therefore people readily embrace them into their lives. It doesn't have to be a romantic relationship. A coworker, friend, or family member can take advantage of someone with these characteristics and manipulate them into their drama. Eventually, a narcissist drops the facade of the perfect (fill in the blank) and their behavior becomes self-serving, to the detriment of others. When their bad behavior is called into question, they utilize the other person's good nature to work against them. They turn the tables and play the victim role: You don't love me, you're being mean to me, you're so insensitive, you always think the worst of me. Today there is a term for that. It is called gaslighting. Unfortunately, I didn't know about that then. When all that fails, a narcissist lies, tells an entirely different version of what just happened, and makes the other person to blame. The other person never realizes they are being manipulated because they are too busy trying to make everything better by being loving, kind, empathetic, and forgiving. It's inherent in their nature and the narcissist takes advantage of it.

The other important characteristic of those preyed on by a narcissist, and the one most significant to my experience, is suffering from low self-esteem. Low self-esteem is rampant in our society. I believe, one of the reasons for that is because when we are developing, we are subject to intense pressures to be the best. The best, which can only be fulfilled by one person, the winner, leaves the rest not feeling good enough. We live in a competitive society where one ultimate winner makes the rest losers. The standards for femininity and masculinity are so narrow and out of reach that only a few can attain and keep them. That implies the rest of us are defective in some way. Wouldn't it be great if we taught cooperation instead of competition and diversity instead of conformity. What if we encouraged children to be the best that they can be instead of just the best? If you had a negative parent, like I did, that drew attention to what's wrong with you and not what is right, the low self-esteem is compounded. I would argue that bullies have low self-esteem and their bullying can lower others self-esteem. I found out early in my life that it not only happens at school when your young, but in all aspects of life. There are bullies in the workplace, sports teams, bars, and of course relationships.

If you are an old soul like me, that has lived many lives as a healer, you probably bring into this life a blueprint to suffer from low self-esteem. It's hardwired into our DNA. This is because healers in the past, even Jesus Christ, have been viewed by their societies as something bad that needed to be eliminated. Whatever the power structure that is in place feels threatened by a healer's unexplainable ability to bring someone into harmony with their bodies and reinstate perfect health. They turn the masses against them by demonizing and calling them witches conducting black magic or acolytes of the devil. They end up being ostracized from their communities or put to death. After this happens for a few lifetimes, the old soul can become imprinted with a belief that there is something wrong with them or they are somehow the perpetrator of their own suffering. Once the imprint is there, they repeat the experience for lifetimes until they awaken to what's going on and clear the imprint from their DNA.

Unfortunately, most of those indicators were present in my life. When I was young, I felt unlovable. I used to chant to myself, "nobody loves me, nobody loves me." My parents were not equipped to have children and were emotionally unavailable. My father was always out drinking with friends in his free time and my mother was too preoccupied with her own unhappiness to be nurturing. They hit all the benchmarks of their generation for parenting; breadwinner and homemaker, to consider themselves good parents, but they weren't very loving. I knew they loved me on some level but not in the emotionally supportive way. My mother was very demanding and negative. Nothing I ever did was good enough. My choices always displeased her. I had two older siblings that were straight-A students that I was constantly compared to. Of course, I was nothing like them. I had trouble learning how to read and barely had a C average. My mother assumed I was stupid and never failed to find an opportunity to remind me of that. She could not have been more wrong. In university, I had to take an IQ test. It turned out my intelligence was just short of genius with a score of 138. I also learned that I was mildly dyslexic hence not grasping the art of reading easily. After hearing those words come out of my mother's mouth daily, the message that I was stupid was implanted in me while I was young and stayed with me well into my forties as I went back to university to obtain a teaching degree. I laughed at myself when I realized I had done that just to prove I wasn't stupid. See mom, I'm a teacher so I can't be stupid! Words are powerful. Choose them carefully. Parents beware.

My childhood experience was made even more challenging because I was a shy, sensitive, loner with no desire to fit in. Bullies saw me as an easy mark that wouldn't fight back. I was picked on and teased unmercifully in grade school for no apparent reason other than I was there. I was also made fun of because I was tall and thin. I grew up believing I was ugly because kids were always pointing at me laughing. The beliefs I grasped onto during my formative years, that I was unattractive and geeky, stayed with me. They were hardwired into my brain. As an adult, life sent me messages that differed from that. I had great friends. I was a leader in action and thought in my own circles. I never had trouble attracting a date if I wanted one.

I even became a successful entrepreneur, partly based on the way I looked. But all of my good times, conquests, and successes never healed me. Deep down, I still felt ugly, stupid, and unlovable. In fact, those beliefs got buried so deeply I forgot they were there.

When I met Mr. Hollywood, I was at a point in my life where I thought I had been in touch with my dark side and healed it. I had read all the books and done all the work to make myself a healthy and happy person living a prosperous life on my own terms. But books can only teach so much. Life is the greatest educator. I needed to have a life experience to remind me of the things I spent a lot of energy to forget. What better venue than a romantic relationship. I was happy being single, so the Universe had to provide something off the charts amazing to get my attention. Mr. Hollywood was bigger than life: Good-looking, charismatic, charming, energetic, and unlike anyone I had come across before. I gravitated towards the unusual and Mr. Hollywood was unique in every way. He was easy to fall in love with and commit to. My big life lesson could not have been wrapped in a more attractive package. Once the Universe had me ensnared in its plan, Mr. Hollywood didn't waste any time in mirroring myself back to me. It was easy for him to do since I came into the relationship feeling like I didn't deserve it. I should have paid more attention to my words. When we were first dating, I expressed disbelief to everybody that somebody like him would be interested in somebody like me. An obvious indicator of low self-esteem that I was oblivious to.

My life with Mr. Hollywood in the desert was barren of everything that contributed to my success back east. All the things that he was originally attracted to. I became something totally different than what I had been when we first met. The small town didn't have a large enough population to make for a successful massage therapy business. Besides, massage therapists were a dime a dozen giving a newcomer a lot of competition. Unlike where I was from, teaching was an extremely low paying profession. All that was required of me wasn't worth the little money I was paid. I no longer made the big money that Mr. Hollywood is attracted to. I ended up doing odd jobs around town to make the money I needed to hold up my end of our financial agreement. It was obvious that Mr. Hollywood was embarrassed in the circles he traveled that I didn't have a big prestige's career anymore. He would make things up about how I made a living. That didn't make me feel very good about myself. I wasn't the big muscle guy any more. The small town we lived in didn't have an adequate gym to keep up with the workouts I was accustomed to. That, compounded with the fact I couldn't be consistent with my program because I was traveling so much resulted in muscle loss. I was still trim and toned but not as bulky as I once was. Eventually, he expressed displeasure with my physicality and told me he wasn't attracted to me anymore. That brought back all my feelings of being ugly and not good enough. He constantly put others' wants, needs, and feelings before mine, making me feel worthless. He wasn't happy with anything I did. I wasn't up to his high-class standards. He never hesitated to express his displeasure. It was like living with my mother all over again. When we would return from a night out, he treated me like I wasn't even there making my head spin because earlier, he had fawned over me like I was his perfect partner. His inconsistency made me question my own sanity. What could I have possibly done to warrant this kind of mistreatment? On some level, did I believe I deserved it?

I have to give Mr. Hollywood credit. He validated beyond any shadow of a doubt that all my hidden beliefs about myself were true. We manifest by our thoughts. Especially our subconscious thoughts. I created somebody to treat me just like I subconsciously believed I should be treated. He became the perfect mirror to me proving that I was unlovable. There is a quote from a book I read while I was figuring this all out. It's called, *The Perks of Being a Wallflower* by

Stephen Chbosky. The quote reads: "We attract the love in our lives we think we deserve." That couldn't have been truer in my case.

My healing process took a long time. It is the hardest thing I have ever done. It seemed like I would take one step forward, then fall two steps back. First, I was paralyzed by my anger. I was indignant. How could he have treated me like this? How could he have lied to me like that? I had a strong need for him to acknowledge what he had done and apologize. Or at least stand in front of me and listen to the long list of indictments I had against him. I don't know why, but I had this need to spew my venom at him and let him know I held him responsible. It took me a while to accept the fact that was never going to happen. From his perspective, he was truly Prince Charming. From what I heard through the grapevine, he readily rewrote the whole relationship, making me the bad guy. Besides, as Dr. Keith had reminded me, he was already into another relationship. I was history. Why would he ever give me the time of day? He would categorically rejected anything I would have said.

I went through a phase where I thought I needed to forgive him. A hard thing to do when the thought of his actions still enraged me. Eventually, after I finally took responsibility for what had happened, the need to forgive was negated. I was the one who went into the relationship with low self-esteem. Mr. Hollywood was the tool of the universe to finally make me aware of it so I could heal it.

The turning point in my healing came when I recognized and honored the relationship with Mr. Hollywood as a gift that gave me an opportunity to get in touch with my buried low self-esteem issues. With that, I was finally able to do deep healing around the seven years we had been together. How could I have ever healed my subconscious views of myself if Mr. Hollywood hadn't mirrored it all back to me? He brought it to the surface so I could become aware of it. Before him, I wasn't even aware I had the issue. I believe, on some astral plane, before Mr. Hollywood and I incarnated, we agreed that he would be the catalyst that would bring this to my attention, giving me an opportunity for me to heal the belief so I could permanently heal and let it go. A soul contract, if you will. We put in place the intense attraction between the two of us to make sure it happened

Now, instead of having to navigate through my anger and hatred if I think of Mr. Hollywood, I am filled with love and gratitude for everything he did for me. If it wasn't for him, I would not be in such a good place about who and what I am now. This is something I have not experienced prior. No longer am I self-deprecating nor deflecting compliments when they come my way. I now graciously accept and show gratitude for the nice words and thoughts people send my way.

Anger and hatred are a huge waste of energy that serves nobody and brings no happiness. It made me miserable for five years. Love and gratitude not only lift up our spirits but bring joy and happiness to the people and the world around us.

It is interesting how perspectives change after beliefs change. It's like looking through an entirely different lens. Historically, I have been my worst critic, comparing myself with everyone around me. I never felt good enough for anything or anyone. I would look at my past and be disappointed. I would analyze old pictures of myself and only see the things I wish could change. Now it is spectacularly different. In the post-mortem of my time spent with Mr. Hollywood, I realized that I was the one who lived honestly and had kept my word to be monogamous. I always treated him like the beautiful soul he is that incarnated into this life as Mr. Hollywood. When I see pictures of the two of us together, I'm surprised that I now think I was the better looking of the two. Even at my worst, I was the one with the better body. I was always the one to be accommodating and supportive. I was able to make enriching and long-lasting friendships with people I met in my new town because I was the one that had a fun, ingratiating, and sincere personality. I know someone else coming from a different place might see things very differently than

I do, and that's okay. What's important to me is for the first time in my life, I felt - and continue to feel - good about myself! I am proud of who I am, what I am, and how I show up in the world.

My healthy self-esteem enables me to finally communicate my thoughts and feelings with self-assuredness and ease. Throughout my life, I rarely spoke up in my relationships because I didn't think my feelings and perspectives had any value. I always deferred to the other person because I felt they were better than me. Now I know differently. How I feel and what I think matters. I share my thoughts and feelings in every situation, not only in relationships, but with friends and in business and social situations too. I am confident in who I am and what I do.

A few weeks after my relationship was over, I was at Pauline's house, the first friend I had made when I moved to Bisbee, exercising my new rage. In my anger, I told her I wished I had never met Mr. Hollywood. She was aghast and immediately corrected me. She pointed out that if I had never met him, I never would have met her, or Susan, or all the other people that I still count as my friends there. She reminded me that it was Susan who helped me take my healing art to all new levels. The town was such a small place. Because of that, I was able to experience what it was like to live in a community where everyone knew each other and helped each other out. Pauline was absolutely right! How could I ever regret any of that? It was all part of the wonderful gift that was Mr. Hollywood. If it wasn't for meeting him, I might still be living in the city I grew up in and not the paradise that I now find myself.

My niece, Lindsey, recently experienced a toxic relationship with a narcissist, and her boyfriend became close with our family. I would watch with difficulty as she checked the same boxes as I had with Mr. Hollywood. I didn't interfere. I recognized it was important for her to have the lesson for herself because I knew it could only be learned through experience. My hope is that those of you who may have experienced something similar can read this and know that you are not crazy, you are not alone, and narcissists cannot and do not desire to change. The only option is to learn and heal yourself.

I have often embraced the knowledge that everything happens for a reason. That belief keeps me from going crazy and leaving the planet. In the beginning, I sometimes felt like the Universe was manipulating me to go down this path with Mr. Hollywood. Now I see it as unavoidable. Yes, I created it. Yes, I chose it each step of the way. Yes, I chose it when I ignored the fact that his rising sign would play out the way it did. Yes, I chose it when I ignored my intuition when it told me he was lying about being ready and wanting a monogamous relationship. Yes, I chose it when I ignored his aberrant behavior in our early travels. I can't deny my complicity in letting the relationship happen. I know my subconscious, my intuitive self, that higher vibration of me knew how important the experience with Mr. Hollywood would be. I needed it to happen so I could get in touch with everything I still needed to heal. If I hadn't healed it, I wouldn't be the person I am today. I wouldn't be evolving to the higher levels I now find myself. I know now that we plan our lives and the people who populate them before we live them. In the planning, we set up certain benchmarks to hit in order to be successful at everything we have set out to accomplish. Nothing can be avoided. When necessary, we build in circumstances that guide us to it. Some experience must happen to get us to where we are going. Death, disaster, pain, suffering, relationships, economic and social events, wars, genocide, crime, and more are often the perfect catalysts to provide us healing and learning that beget growth, evolution, and happiness. Everything has purpose and meaning and it's all playing out perfectly according to our divine plan. We should always look for the beauty in it. Life always gives you what you need, not necessarily what you want. If we don't achieve our goals the first time around, we get infinite opportunities to succeed until we do. It never ends. If you don't do it in this life, you will have to do it in the next. Some things are just unavoidable.

L ESSON LEARNED!

Starman

Back in Cleveland I was working as a massage therapist at Dr. Keith's clinic while I was waiting for the house in the desert to sell. When I finished with a massage, I always left the room to give the client a moment to recover and get dressed. While I waited, I would walk up to the front desk and hang out with the receptionist. One afternoon, when I arrived at the desk, the customer that was checking out turned and looked at me. Without hesitation she declared that I was an Angel. The Archangel Michael to be exact. I got that a lot over the years given my clear blue eyes and long wavy blonde hair framing my face that others have described as sweet and innocent. Jane, the other massage therapist that I had befriended, looked up from behind the desk where she was updating a chart and assertively corrected the woman and informed her that I was a Starman. I don't know who was more surprised, the client or me. I had never heard of a Starman before. The customer didn't like being contradicted. She quickly finished her transaction and left the building without saying another word. I watched while she walked out the door. When she was gone, I turned back to the desk, looked at Jane who was standing there with an mischievous smile on her face and asked her what a Starman was.

Science Fiction movies became popular in the 50s and 60s. I grew up in a culture that treated aliens as a reality not a possibility. I remember watching programs like *Star Trek* and *Lost in Space*. The writers created imaginative stories that reinforced the idea of different worlds populated with unusual beings. Often, they were portrayed as benevolent. Seeds of curiosity and wonder were planted. UFO sightings were constantly in the news and alien abductions were weekly headlines on the gossip racks in the supermarket checkout line. There was never a question in my mind that other beings from different worlds existed. How could they not? The universe is vast with billions of known galaxies and continues to grow as our technology improves to discover and map it all out. The Milky Way Galaxy which our solar system circulates in is a small pinprick of a place in the immensity of the universe. I have often thought it was arrogant for men to think that Earth was the only planet that had intelligent life, with all that possibility. I did question why books and movies demonized other civilizations as something we needed to fear because they were going to take over the planet. In my mind, if other life forces or aliens had the technology for space travel, they would have more advanced societies than the ones we had on Earth. What would they want with us? The cultures that mankind has created thus far are primitive. I imagined an evolved society would foster love, compassion, community, and equality thus creating a utopia where the power structures served its citizens rather than enslaving them. What I grew up with on Earth was the total opposite. Our cultures, for the most part, pander to greedy leaders that create fear amongst the masses to ensure their ability to maintain power. They promote hatred for one another to fuel a war machine that makes the rich richer. Divide and conquer is their mantra. As a burgeoning healer, I see our "drug and cut" medical industry as another extension of that greed which preys upon the forced ignorance of the people they are meant to be serving. I surmised that a visit from some aliens could only be a good thing.

I read the book *Chariots of the Gods* by Erich von Däniken as a teenager. He used evidence from ancient archaeological sites to hypothesize that our planet was visited by astronauts from other planets which helped advance the human race both genetically and technologically. I loved the many photos of primitive art depicting space men and flying airships. I found it fascinating and convincing. My intuition concurred. After reading it, I was left with the feeling that visits from extraterrestrials were continuing to this day. A decade later, Shirley MacLaine became the purveyor of the New Age spiritual revolution by sharing her various personal mystical experiences and her belief in reincarnation and channeling. In her book *Out on a Limb*, Ms. MacLaine writes extensively about UFO sightings in South America which were common in the 70's and 80's. Exposure to her and other media that touched on the topic, left me totally open and accepting of the idea that the human race on Earth is being guided and genetically enhanced to facilitate a huge evolutionary leap in human consciousness. This will usher in and support the Golden Age on Earth that has been prophesied.

Enter the idea of Starman. The day after the incident with the patient at the clinic, Jane gave me a little pocket-sized book that talked about various Starmen and their different qualities. I'm sorry to say, I have no memory of the name of the book. I only had it for one night before I gave it back to Jane the following day. It was an interesting read naming different planetary systems in different galaxies, all known to man, and the qualities of the races that inhabited them. It affirmed that at one time or another all of these races had intervened on Earth and over time facilitated human evolution in their own unique way which continues to this day. A soul from one of these places can agree to incarnate as a human on Earth bringing with them an innate knowledge from their original culture in order to seed earthlings' consciousness and help the advancement of the human race. Yes, aliens walk among us.

I will give a brief description of a few of them:

- Sirians are from the planets Sirius A and Sirius B. They are blue light beings that serve as a nexus point and way station for the ultimate transcendence of our consciousness.

- Andromedans are from the Andromeda Galaxy. They bring peace and love to the races around the universe. They are heart-centered and noted for having perfect balance between the two hemispheres of the brain.
- Orionians are from the planet Orion. They are detail-oriented intellects who question everything. They excel at science and research and are here to improve our knowledge of it. Unfortunately, they are not very emotional.
- Arcturions are from Arcturus. They are multidimensional beings modeling a prototype for life on Earth that moves through the different dimensions easily. They are mentally and emotionally advanced and become shamans and healers of humanity.

When I read about the Pleiadian Starmen I was stunned, if not shocked to my very core! It explained everything I had known about myself and made sense of my entire experience on the planet! Pleiadians are from the Pleiades, a star system of seven major planets that can be seen in Earth's night sky. In the Native American cultures, they were referred to as the Seven Sisters. The story goes that the seven sisters are fed up with their husbands (all brothers) not sharing with them their game so they asked to be changed into stars. Some of the Pleiades are water worlds so it is common to find Pleiadians close to water. The markings they manifest as humans are tall, thin bodies because they are always reaching up to the stars in the sky. They usually have blue eyes and blonde hair that frame heart shaped faces with high cheekbones and strong chins. Metabolically, they have low blood pressure, body temperature and heart rates. They chose to be born into dysfunctional situations to help heal generational family issues of addiction, trauma, and abuse. Of course, they are so different from their birth families that they don't feel like they fit in and often become the black sheep of the family because they can't be anything but what they are. They often engage in various forms of escapism because they intuitively know that the Earth is not their native planet. They present themselves to the world as charming, sensual, and magnetic with an ethereal presence. For those that can see it, they radiate bright, light blue auras. Nurturing and healing come naturally to them, and they are always helping people. They end up working in some capacity of service. Empathetic by nature, they often give too much of themselves and easily attract narcissists. Natural pacifists, they refuse to fight or engage in any kind of violence as they hold to an idealistic view of the world. Instead, they are diplomatic when in a disagreement. They intuitively know from the start that they are here on a mission or with a purpose. Pleidians are incarnating on Earth to assist in the awakening that is currently happening on the planet by helping people open up their hearts to love. What was so stunning to me as I read through the description was the fact you could substitute my name for Pleidian and everything would be true. Suddenly I knew who I was, where I was from, and why I was so different. I imagine the comfort I felt finding this out might be what an adopted child feels like when they find their biological parents.

Everything came into focus. Things that I thought or believed all made sense in the context of being a Pleidian Starman from a more advanced culture. I remember walking home from school when I was a kid and seeing the moon in the bright afternoon sky which occurs when it is waxing into a full moon. Before I understood the rotation of the moon, I couldn't understand why it could be seen during the day when the moon was a night feature. What really struck me while looking up at the moon was that there weren't more orbs in the afternoon sky. I could easily imagine three at various distances and sizes. I also thought the color of the sky should be a light lemon yellow and not blue. When you think about the Pleiades being so close together, I bet if you are standing on one planet you could see some of the other planets in the sky at all times. I know from Earth Science studies that the color of the sky is contingent on the atmosphere. I wonder what the atmospheric conditions are on the planets of the Pleiades. Maybe they do have yellow skies. I can't wait to go home and find out.

I knew my suicidal inclinations had to originate from somewhere. It was odd being so young at five years of age or earlier, and feeling the way that I did. I assumed it was something I brought in from a past life, which in a way I did, but being a Starman from the Pleiades put a whole different light on the situation. It must have made coming to the primitive planet of Earth difficult. I was probably horrified by what I was witnessing and just wanted to go home. I definitely didn't relate to my parents and my two brothers. I had nothing in common with any of them. I looked at everything totally differently than they did. I do have a sister that I have always been close to. When I told Sandra about being a Starman, she surprised me and said that she thought she was one too. After I thought about it made perfect sense. She always exhibited immense empathy and compassion. She worked as a nurse, a healer in her own right. And she possessed a strong desire to be of service in any way. I guess that explained why we always "got" one another. I brought with me a memory of what a loving, civilized society was. Of course, I would be appalled by the human race treating each other so badly with their wars, power grabs, greedy accumulation of goods causing shortages elsewhere, the suppression of the masses, and violence consuming institutions on Earth. It was innately unacceptable to me. I knew it needed to be healed and changed. I never let go of my utopian ideal of what life on Earth could and should be, in my eyes. It makes sense that as a child, I wanted out.

The most meaningful and significant revelation about my origins was my desire to be a healer. That is what Pleidians are most noted for with their empathy and desire to help others and living a life of service. It is my deep empathy that enables me to intuitively feel others' pain and understand their experience from their view. It's probably why just about everything makes me cry, happy or sad. My family and friends have always teased me about my waterworks that flow so easily. I can't help it. I become overwhelmed by the emotion, in the moment, alongside whoever is having the experience as if I was actually having the experience too. It is no wonder I aspired to be a healer. It's what Pleidians do.

The most famous Pleidian and healer that has incarnated on Earth was Jesus Christ. Yes, he was a Starman. He came to model what a more advanced culture could be. His appearance may have been different then the markers I listed earlier for Pleidians because of the middle eastern culture he chose to be born into, but his every act and word emanated from the deep compassion and empathy inherent in Pleidians. He used the superior science and technology of his world to perform what humans saw as miracles. What he did, using the power of his mind and knowing that he could create anything he chose, was change the vibration of a thing or a disease using quantum physics. This enabled him to walk on water, turn water into wine, and heal the infirmed. Our science today is beginning to prove that this will be the future in the healing arts and the solution to many other problems that plague the Earth today. Everything Jesus Christ embodied are Pleidian qualities. Including unconditional love, non-judgment, honesty, pacifism, tolerance, selflessness, charity - and of course - being a compassionate and empathetic healer who was living a life of service.

I'm not a religious person nor do I consider myself a Christian. My focus has always been on spirituality that comes from within. With that said, Jesus and I have a history.

I continued my personal healing while I was living in the desert. A friend told me about an energetic healer in the next town over. I decided to pursue him about a chronic shoulder issue I was having. His name was Jerry. He had no particular degree that I knew of, just an ability to read auras and feel energy blocks that he was able to move out. I was very impressed with the results I experienced from my first session with him, so I made a second appointment.

Between my first and second session with Jerry, I had a philosophical debate with someone about being a healer. It centered around the idea that if someone held the power to perform miracles and heal people, were they obligated to use that gift. I said yes. How could you choose to not end people's suffering if you possessed the power to do so. What good is a gift like that if you never share it? The other person said no. A person is never obligated to do anything they don't want to do. We have free will at all times and the choice is always ours without judgements. The other part of the debate was about whether or not we have the right to deny somebody a learning experience that a disease might facilitate. My friend and I both agreed on this point. Nobody has the right to make decisions for somebody else. Whoever is being helped has to be complicit and agree to the healing. I always start my healing work by asking my client if I have permission to work on them.

At the second session, I told Jerry about the debate and asked his opinion as a healer. He agreed with my friend. Being a healer was not an obligation. I began to explain my position when Jerry stopped me mid-sentence and asked me to wait a minute while he got my file. He said that he wanted me to read something he had written after my first session. He was gone just a minute when it hit me. Without any indication from him, I was certain of what he was going to show me. I had never been surer of anything before in my life. I sat on the edge of the examination table with my feet dangling off the edge gently kicking the side of the table. I was trying not to cry from all the emotion that was overwhelming me. He came back into the room with my folder neatly opened between his hands. Without saying a word, he pointed to the words written on the page. It read "I met Jesus Christ today." I couldn't control myself any longer and started sobbing uncontrollably. What I was feeling and why I was crying, I cannot express. A thousand emotions washed over me all at once. When I was able to catch my breath, I told him of my premonition of what he was about to show me. I explained that on some level, I had always felt that to be true in some way. He didn't seem surprised, nor did he think it was odd. He couldn't explain why, but for some reason, incarnations of people from the story of Jesus were showing up in this desert area. He said he already had met two other participants in the story. I was the third.

I asked Jerry that if I truly was Jesus Christ, why wasn't I performing miracles? A constant frustration of mine. He said that I was blocking my abilities, as many lightworkers do, because in past lives, every time I used them, it ended badly. He added with a chuckle that if I used them in this life, it would end badly too. I was confused and asked him to explain. He pointed out that Jesus was crucified for being a healer. He added that I had reincarnated many times as a healer since then and each time it brought me to some horrible end because the people in power were threatened by it. He laughed and said after being put to death so many times, I had learned my lesson and kept myself hidden. I had to laugh at that too.

It felt good to finally have someone to talk to about all this without fear of being judged negatively or thought insane. He treated this like it was the most normal thing in the world. It also helped that he had a sense of humor about it.

145

This new information was a real mindfuck! I grappled with it for a couple of years and discussed it with countless people. Most people didn't buy into the idea that I was the actual reincarnation of Jesus himself but that I embodied, as many people do, the essence of Jesus. That felt right to me. I did, and do, try to model Jesus and live my life accordingly.

Most people see their body, mind, and soul and their present Earthly experience as separate from everything else. It is their unique, individual expression. This has been necessary up until now in order to function on the Earth plane. When a soul is born, the veil keeps hidden their true connection with the universe. As the human race slowly opens up to a higher understanding of our experience, we have come to know that we are all one. How can that be? For me, this is the divine mystery and it takes a little faith to help wrap my mind around it. Whatever you may call it - the Divine energy, the Creator, or God - it was all present in the beginning. It wanted to experience itself, so it started splitting into an infinite number of facets in order to have different experiences of all that it was while remaining the ultimate One. All of these new facets consist of an infinite number of pieces too. This becomes so complicated; I have trouble wrapping my mind around it. All these different facets enable a soul to live their lives simultaneously because on higher dimensional levels time doesn't exist. Everything is happening in the eternal moment of now. All lives, past, present, and future occur simultaneously.

Time was invented to organize and coordinate day and night, project planting cycles, and regulate work or ritual events. Later it was used to record and measure the movement of the planets and the progression of the seasons, but at its most basic definition it is just a perceived distance between two things happening.

Using me as an example, I have my focus in this life on Earth while I am aware that there are an infinite number of unique experiences of myself happening all at the same time, all over the universe having focused lives of their own simultaneously. As I embrace the belief that we are all one, I acknowledge that a piece of me is also shared with the facet of me having the Jesus experience which also happens to be a focus of mine in my current life. Imagine the complexity when you factor in the infinite number of beings in the universe doing this simultaneously. In essence, this basic, over simplified explanation becomes the definition of the Divine energy, the Creator, or God, whichever descriptor you prefer, experiencing itself.

It is not uncommon for new people I meet to connect me with Jesus or the Jesus energy. After my house in Bisbee sold, I ended up on the west coast of Florida in the Tampa Bay area. I spent a month looking at various possibilities of where to live. My first weekend in St. Petersburg, I met a woman named Tracy who was a friend of somebody who was hitting on me in a bar. The guy ended up being a jerk, but Tracy and I had an instant connection. On the night we met she happened to have in her bag a deck of cards similar to a Tarot deck. She had me pull a card. Of course, I pulled the one associated with Jesus. She wasn't surprised. She then pulled out a book and read something related to Jesus in reference to him being a Starman. I expressed my surprise and excitement that she was looking at him from that perspective. It seems when I get a new level of understanding about something, I receive confirmation multiple times from various sources. She explained that she herself is a Blue Star Sirian Starman from Sirius B. It was like I found my long-lost family! Somebody who understood my experience without explanation. It felt good.

I ended up choosing to move to St. Petersburg, commonly referred to as St. Pete, or it chose me. Three weeks later I was driving my new car packed with my belongings stored in Cleveland at mom's down to my new home in Florida. I rendezvoused with my best friend Kris in Asheville, North Carolina at a wonderfully authentic tea house that had intricate carved wooden partitions, colorful Moroccan tapestries, and abundant pillows everywhere. The fragrant scent of exotic teas overcame me as soon as I walked through the door. There was only one other customer there, a woman sitting two tables away. She overheard our conversation about my moving to St. Pete. Without invitation she joined us and excitedly explained that St. Pete was one of three energy vortexes in North America that were stabilizing the grid during the transition into the Aquarian Age. The other two are located at Mt. Shasta in northern California and in Sedona, Arizona. She was definitely a kindred spirit. She quickly steered the conversation to astrology and asked us our Astro information. She must have had psychic abilities as well because when she gave us her assessment of us, she was spot on with both Kris and myself and our current spiritual paths. There was something not of this Earth about her. I have often wondered if she was a Starman too and was at the tea house on purpose waiting for me to provide guidance. If I had any doubts about my decision to move to St. Pete, she erased them. I am constantly amazed when synchronicity appears in my life with people, places, and things showing up at just the right time. Life may appear to be random but as I stated earlier, everything happens for a reason.

Tracy introduced me to the unusually large and welcoming spiritual community in St. Pete. Everywhere I went, I was greeted with some sort of reference to my connection with Jesus. It didn't hurt that I had long blonde hair and a trimmed goatee at the time. I even reminded myself of the western version of Jesus when I looked in the mirror. Coincidence? I learned that the many miles of white seashore running up and down the west coast of Florida are made of quartz sand. No wonder this was an energy vortex. All that quartz holds vibration. My favorite spiritual community was - and still is - Sacred Lands, which was only a few miles from where I live. It is maintained by the Anderson family on the site of an old Native

American village that the Spaniards landed in the 1400's. There are still Indian mounds there that can be viewed. As soon as you step foot on the property, you can feel the holiness of it. The community offers discussion groups, solstice and equinox ceremonies, meditation groups, coffee houses, and a Kirtan, devotional singing in Sikhism, music coffee house on Sunday evenings. I have never lived anywhere before where experiences like this were common. It was easy to be out of the spiritual closet in St. Pete. I could be open about my spirituality and share my views of the universe and be totally accepted without judgment. It was refreshing, to say the least.

Many authors, astrologers, and channelers talk about the role of Pleiadians in the evolution of the human race on Earth. They are referred to as our unseen ancestors. There is a consensus that the Pleiadians arrived to help seed our race with a goal of upgrading our primitive brains to a level where we can process and assimilate a higher level of thinking. It is also thought that Pleiadians interbreed with our race to change the number of chromosomes from the usual 24 pairs in the animal kingdom to the unique 23 pairs of chromosomes which only humans have. They also shared their DNA separating us even further from the animal kingdom and bringing us closer to our divinity. There is a consistent story in indigenous cultures that there was some sort of intervention that enabled humans to make an evolutionary leap. Scientists have hypothesized that this evolutionary leap happened 200,000 years ago. Scientists can't explain why it happened; they just know that it did. Pleiadian intervention could explain the evolutionary leaps that mankind has made in ancient times which birthed entirely new and different cultures and civilizations here on Earth. This has no other explanation for this evolutionary leap except that it suddenly appeared. It could be said that humans are a hybrid of Pleiadians.

In relation to our 23 sets of chromosomes, I recently read that there is a 24th pair that is energetic that hasn't been activated yet. It is invisible to the human eye and hasn't been detected by the science that presently exists. Its ultimate activation will enable humans to function in multidimensions making it easy for us to move from one dimension to another. Technology will soon be invented to measure and prove its existence.

I find these topics difficult to write about because it may appear far-fetched to those who haven't heard about it before. The word "esoteric" applies here. It means, known by only a few. I admit I am not the expert on any of this. There are many resources available that give a better explanation of how this will all play out. Let me assure all the readers that when I am advancing my own understanding and I see the same information presented the same way from different sources countless times, I have learned to embrace it when it intuitively feels right.

This feels very right to me!

Pleiadian's are also relatively low on the evolutionary ladder when you take into consideration all of the inhabitants of the universe, but they are eons ahead of humans on Earth. When a soul awakens and begins to evolve, they start to understand the "oneness" of the Universe. All souls, from whatever part of the universe, on some level know that we are all in this together. What we do for one, we do for the collective. The human race is on the verge of understanding and embracing this wisdom. Pleiadian's are intervening in any way possible without doing the actual work for us. They teach and elevate through modeling the more highly evolved qualities of unconditional love, non-judgment, honesty, pacifism, tolerance, self-lessness, charity, compassion, and empathy. Jesus was such a model exhibiting these qualities consistently throughout his life. Pleiadian's were helped on their evolutionary path and now are helping the human race the same way they were helped. I'm reminded of the movie *Pay It Forward;* instead of paying a person back who did you a good deed, you pass it on to another person instead. The Pleiadians are paying it forward just like Earthlings will pay it forward for the next planet with an emerging evolving race. The divine plan is beautiful in its simplicity.

If you want to read more about the Pleiadians, where they come from, who they are, and their role in our evolution, I highly suggest you pursue the many wonderful books written by Barbara Marciniak.

The Earth plane, and those inhabiting it, are living through the most extraordinary and powerful energetic and evolutionary leap that life on this planet has ever experienced thus far. Galactics from all over the universe are here either physically or energetically to assist in the transformation of the human race. Starmen from across the universe are incarnating now on our planet to share their wisdom, knowledge, and science to help take us to the next level on the evolutionary ladder. As the light becomes brighter and the darkness is exposed, it will be safe for them to disseminate their particular gifts to the masses, without concern that the advanced technology could be used for violence or war. Everything that is being gifted is done in the name of unconditional love, peace, and evolution.

WE ARE NOT ALONE

Russ, Is That You?!

St. Petersburg, Florida is the first place I have lived that I cannot imagine ever leaving. I live in a small complex that backs onto Boca Ciega Bay. There is a nicely landscaped yard and a dock to sit on facing a marina where the sun rises each morning. When I cross the street in the other direction, I am literally on one of the most beautiful beaches in the world with its white quartz sand that never gets too hot to walk barefoot on. I go there most evenings to watch the sunset and do my affirmations. It fits my personal definition of living in paradise. Having access to the beach daily makes me feel like the luckiest man in the world. I support myself by doing which I love. My work has always been my passion. I learned long ago that working for other people or corporations doesn't make me happy. I need my autonomy. By doing an occasional massage and my healing work as a Medical Intuitive, I make enough money to get by but not much more. My clients are wonderful souls that are interested in health, spirituality, and their personal growth. It is an honor to be a facilitator for them. For the most part life is good and I am happy.

I didn't date anyone for two years after Mr. Hollywood. I wasn't in a very good space mentally or spiritually. I know through the laws of attraction that we are magnets for what we are and the energy we are projecting. The thought of what I would draw into my life at that point was pretty scary. As I started to heal, I slowly began to entertain the idea that there might be another love in my life, someone I could spend my golden years with. After all, the astrologer that worked on me at the dinner party when I was 40 predicted I was going to be hit by love one last time when I was 58 years old. It was fun to think that I may be blessed with magic again.

The first guy I dated was the total opposite of narcissistic. I try not to repeat the same mistake twice. Unfortunately, he was a little too out of control and needy with some health issues that interfered with what I would prefer for a life partner. I also think he might have been an alcoholic and abusing drugs. He lived 45 minutes away so I didn't spend enough time with him to figure it out for sure. We had a lot of fun together, but I lost interest after a year or so.

After that, I was totally open to possibilities and started dating in earnest, but nothing ever lasted more than a couple of months. The years passed by without much notice. I found myself quickly approaching my 59th birthday and beginning to think the astrologer may have had it wrong. Honestly, I was coming to terms with the strong possibility of living the rest of my life as a bachelor. Even though I was living an amazing life with family and friends and enjoying the moments, I missed having a romantic special someone to share life with. Being single was great and definitely had its advantages, but now that I was older, I had to admit life was more fun when I had someone to share it with. The idea of a solo life that was getting me depressed. I could feel myself sliding into one of my black holes which still happened occasionally.

I had fallen into a morning routine over the years. I would get up and drink lots of water then get back into bed with my computer to give my body time to rehydrate before I got up to do my morning yoga. I would always glance at the news, check the weather (which is generally a waste of time for us Floridians), look at my emails, and finish up by perusing Facebook.

There usually wasn't much to look at on Facebook. I got in the habit of scrolling through pretty fast to avoid the endless "suggestions for you" posts. One morning while scrolling, the face of a man flashed before my eyes. In that brief microsecond the photo was on the computer screen, I saw something. I worked my way back to the post to get a better look. Staring out from the computer was the most handsome man I had ever seen. I stared at the picture for the longest time thinking he was my perfect ideal of male beauty and masculinity. There was something about his soulful eyes that kept me riveted. His big toothy smile framed by deeply entrenched dimples helped to keep my attention too. Minutes ticked by. As I looked at the picture, I surrendered to my depression. At that moment I believed I was too old to attract somebody that young and good looking. Somebody like him wouldn't give me the time of day. I was wrongfully buying into the belief of aging and thought my shelf life as a desirable partner had come and gone. That Love Boat had sailed, and I was left standing at the dock.

As an afterthought, I read what was written above the picture. The man was looking for a place to rent. I fervently wished I had a house with an extra room. I would have rented it to him in a New York minute just to be able to admire him every day.

Later that day, I found myself downtown running errands. It was getting late in the afternoon and I needed a break. I decided to chill at one of the outdoor tables at a coffee house and people watch for a while. Always a fun pastime. All the tables where I usually sat on the shady side of the building were occupied. I couldn't ever remember that happening before. I went around the corner and found two more tables that were shaded only by their umbrellas. There was a man sitting at one of the tables facing towards the building playing on his phone with a headset covering his ears. The other table was miraculously empty. I quickly made it my own. I sat down facing out so I could see the pedestrians pass by. It took me about ten minutes to notice that the man sitting at the next table had huge thighs. I thought to myself that with thighs like that he had to have a nice ass, my favorite part of the male anatomy. As soon as I thought that, I looked up to find the man was staring right at me while I was checking his thighs out. He flashed me a big smile with insanely cute dimples. I must have turned three shades of red in embarrassment and quickly looked away. I sat there and ignored him while I tried to regain my composure before I continued on with my errands.

Something stopped me from getting up and going. I kept thinking that the man looked familiar. He was engrossed in his phone again and didn't notice I was looking at him out of the corner of my eye. I sat there trying to place where I might know him from. It took me a while to figure it out. When I did, it marked the point where, for the first time in my life, I totally lost control of myself. Something inexplicable took over me. I whipped around in my seat and rapped on his table top to get his attention. As soon as he took off his headset, I blurted out, "Did you post something on Facebook this morning?" Unbelievably, it was the guy I was mooning over just a few hours earlier! What were the odds that I would sit next to him that afternoon. Serendipity was working overtime. Some things are just meant to be.

My outburst turned out to be the perfect ice breaker. He laughed and flashed me those deep pools of dimples again. He clarified that the post I had seen that morning was in fact his. His name was Breck. I had never heard that name before. I liked it. I asked him how his rental search was going and he admitted it was not going very well. After I remembered to introduce myself, I told him my story of seeing him on Facebook earlier that day. He was as amazed about the coincidence as I was. I inquired on how he found himself in this current situation. He told me a brief story of a failed romance. I quipped that such events always seemed to be the case and we had a good laugh. One thing led to another and before I knew it, we had garnered a brief history of each other's lives and how we both had ended up in St. Pete.

We had an instant connection and familiar rapport with one another. The conversation flowed easily. We started saying things at the same time which made us both uncomfortable. Before long we were finishing each other's sentences. My emotions were spiking off the charts. I never wanted the moment to end. I asked him if he would like to come home with me. I couldn't believe my own ears when I heard the words coming out of my mouth. I was so out of control. I had never done anything like that before. I was responding without thinking. A totally alien experience for someone like me who always analyzes and overthinks everything before acting.

At home back on the beach, I proudly showed him my condo and asked him to stay for dinner so we could continue to get to know each other. He had a Chinese character tattooed on his upper arm. I asked him what it meant. He told me the symbol meant family. He had decided to get the tattoo because he was looking for his family. Not his biological one. He told me he had stopped talking to them when he left home at the age of 18. He had been on his own ever since. He was searching for people that would accept and love him unconditionally that would come together and create a family where he felt he belonged. Without missing a beat, I earnestly looked him in the eye and informed him he had just found it. I think I was more surprised that those words came out of my mouth than he was. He happily nodded in agreement as tears rolled down his cheeks. Finally, somebody who felt his emotions like I did. It didn't take me long to join in with the waterworks. We sat staring into each other's eyes for the longest time, tears running down our cheeks, lovingly grinning in recognition.

Now for the big question. I couldn't believe I had restrained myself as long as I had. I explained that I was into astrology and that I was curious what sign he was. He immediately told me he was an Aquarian, my astrological complement. I told him the astrology I wanted to do was a little more in depth as I started up my computer to pull up my favorite astrology site. I asked him if he could give me the day, time, and place of his birth. Surprisingly, he knew it all. I hesitated when he gave me the year as 1995. While I was inputting the birth info, I quickly did the math in my head. I almost fell out of my chair when I realized he was only 23 years old! I looked at the man sitting across from me. I never would have guessed he was that young. He had a mature masculinity about him with his big muscular frame, mustache, and lambchop sideburns.

I did my best not to show my surprise. I averted his gaze while I processed this new revelation. I focused on the computer screen and finished entering his birth info into the astrology site. It turned out that he was a triple Aquarian meaning the big three (sun, rising, and moon) were all in Aquarius. I read out loud the description for each. I could tell by his reaction that what I recited resonated strongly with him. I was happy with what I read too. I pointed out to him that Aquarius is directly opposite my sign of Leo on the astrological wheel. I explained that it made us total opposites and that opposites attract. Like two magnets, we were drawn to each other. Breck liked the attraction part but was uncomfortable with the idea that we were total opposites. I assured him it was a good thing. I explained that between the two of us, we had it all. He smiled again, flashing me those big dimples. His smile was infectious. I couldn't help but burst into one as well.

I never mentioned his age. In truth, I didn't know what to say about that. To Breck's credit, he never asked about my age either. I assumed we were both silently complicit to ignore the obvious. He eventually shared with me years later that he thought I was in my forties the day we met. I laughed and told him I thought he was in his thirties. Interesting how the universe works.

I never formally asked Breck to spend the night, he just did. In fact, he has spent every night with me since the day we met. I think it's romantic that we have never spent a night apart. Our relationship and cohabitation happened without forethought or planning. It didn't take us long to fall into a comfortable daily routine. We had common interests like bodybuilding, dancing, movies, and food, which we enjoyed together. We were very much in sync with one another. I noticed at the gym between sets we would slightly sway in unison together as we talked. There was no real explanation for our relationship. The way we came together was beyond destiny; it seemed inevitable. It was more like we had always been together and always would be. As if, we had been on a short break before we had found each other again.

We spent a lot of time staring into each other's eyes. I found his hypnotic. I could see everything in the depths of his dark brown eyes; all that he was and all that he will be for eternity. I always felt the eyes were the window to the soul. When I look into somebody's eyes, I feel a connection being made. I'm acutely aware that there is a distinct entity inside the human whose eyes I'm staring into. An energy - the soul - that knows the past and the future. A soul possessing all the wisdom of the universe reflecting everything that I am back to me. This happens when I stare into my own eyes in a mirror too. I'm seeing the me that is independent of my body. When I lovingly stared into Breck's eyes, I saw all this and something more. I couldn't put my finger on it, but it felt very familiar.

I learned over time that Breck had a tough childhood. When he was one and a half, his mother left him and his two sisters in the care of his father and never returned. He grew up in poor and lived in dangerous neighborhoods where the threat of violence was always present. He shared a story that he witnessed a friend of his being shot and dying. I didn't know what to do with that information. I had no frame of reference. That was so far from my reality that I couldn't relate. His father was away working a lot but when he was home, he was disapproving of Breck's love for acting and singing and was verbally abusive. He wanted his son to be a man's man, forcing him to play sports that Breck had no interest in. His father and extended family were devout Jehovah's Witnesses. They never celebrated holidays or birthdays. Breck had to spend much of his free time with the family at church events. The church denounced Breck for his love of dance, his love of music and for his sexuality publicly condemning him as a sinner. All these experiences were damaging and Breck suffers from them to this day. After high school, Breck was forced to go to college. That lasted one semester. Breck was definitely not college material. Father and son got into a heated argument over his returning to school which ended with Breck leaving home for good. Sadly, Breck refuses to have anything to do with his controlling, disapproving family to this day. Probably not a bad thing.

We spent most of our time sitting at the dining room table. Beyond the dining room is a hallway that leads to the bathroom and sleeping quarters. I use the walls of the hallway as a photo gallery for all the people that have made a difference in my life by helping me evolve into the man I am today. I think it is important to live in gratitude for them. Their photos are my daily reminder of how blessed I have been.

Of course, one of those people framed on the wall is Russ. From my position sitting at the table, I can clearly see his picture hanging on the wall. One morning I was sitting there looking at Breck when I noticed I could see Russ's face staring back at me, simultaneously. I looked from one to the other and started to notice the many similarities between the two's facial features. I was amazed at how much they looked alike. They had the same eyes, nose, and mouth on a similarly shaped face. The only real difference was the hair and Russ's dimples weren't as pronounced. One could easily mistake them for the same person. I chuckled to myself when I realized I clearly have "a type."

The resemblance had me thinking. The more I thought about it, Breck was like Russ in other ways too. My mind started to wander. It hopped from one coincidence or similarity to another. My mind, or soul, was trying to get somewhere but I didn't know where. Suddenly, it hit me! I needed to find out what year Russ passed. Russ was born within a few days of my older brother which made it easy to remember his birthday. Apparently, our mothers were in the maternity ward at the same time giving birth. I knew that Russ passed away when he was 42 years old. I did some quick math adding 42 to the year my brother was born and determined that he passed in 1995. That year felt so familiar. What was it about 1995 that made it significant? Sometimes it takes me a little while before all the pieces fall into place. When the light bulb finally turned on, it took everything in my power not to react in front of Breck. Russ passed the same year Breck was born!

My mind instantly started questioning the probability that Russ and Breck were of the same soul. I never said a word to Breck about my suspicions. How do you tell your new partner that he is somebody you knew earlier in life? I never wanted Breck to feel like I love him because I thought he was somebody else. Breck is definitely a unique individual separate from Russ and our current relationship is specific to Breck and me. It definitely has its own dynamic except for one big issue. Drug use. Russ's use of mescaline was the reason why I wouldn't open up to a relationship with him. Breck uses marijuana. It's not something I would want in my life but I choose to tolerate it. I have changed. I'm not the same person I was when I was in my twenties. I thought about this constantly for weeks on end, trying to dismiss the notion that they were one and the same souls. The more I thought about it, the probability that they were, grew stronger in my head.

It was so much more than the two looking alike or the coincidence of Russ leaving the planet and Breck arriving on the planet in the same year; although that seemed to be the clincher. Their circumstances and challenges in life were similar. Russ and Breck grew up in very similar circumstances of poverty in dysfunctional, abusive families that they excommunicated at an early age leaving them to battle low self-esteem, lack of confidence, and anger issues. These were coupled with streaks of violence and a distinct belief that the world owed them something for their hardships. They both used drugs to take the edge off their disappointments: Russ mescaline and Breck marijuana. They both possessed artistic talents and aspired to make it in the arts. Russ was a visual artist focusing on photography. Breck's desire is to be an entertainer who uses his deep voice to make it in the music industry. Each of them longed to find new families where they would be loved and accepted unconditionally creating a safe environment for them to open up and return that affection with their immeasurable capacity to bestow love without fear of rejection. In their own way, each had saved me from my own self-destructive suicidal tendencies. In addition, there were many small similarities that were constantly catching my attention that reinforced the idea that Breck was Russ reincarnated.

The next thing I had to ask myself was: What was my role in all this? If my reincarnation theory was true, I had attracted a relationship twice with the same soul. Was it because I was to help them in some way or that I was supposed to learn something that I missed the first time around? Certainly, I am a much different person with new tools and abilities that I wasn't equipped with earlier in my life. Russ had dreamt of being in a committed relationship with me and did everything in his power to make it happen. I knew he loved me deeply but I consciously rejected him to keep myself safe from all the issues that Russ brought with him. In that respect, I failed him completely by affirming all his beliefs that he was unlovable with my unwillingness to open up and take a chance and love someone unconditionally. There is no doubt in my mind that my actions contributed to his beliefs about himself that eventually manifested his cancer experience. Was this my second chance to get it right and open up in the context of a relationship to help him heal and evolve so he could move on to other things? As my relationship plays out with Breck, it appears that way.

At this point in my life, I am able to accept people and situations for what they are without judgment or making it personal and to simply be a point of love and light for them. I now have the ability to look at a situation and see why it is the way it is and respond accordingly. I have watched Breck transform from a scared, hurt person who used anger to protect himself into someone who is more confident and empowered. This has enabled him to lower his defenses and be more open in social situations. This helps him be more proactive in making his personal dreams come true. He is infinitely more forgiving, which defuses his anger at things he has no control over. The old axiom, "Love heals all wounds," exists for a reason. Because, it's true! I let down all of my defenses, barriers, judgments and assumptions, and opened up my heart to Breck letting my unconditional love bath him in acceptance, understanding, and support. At times, when he thought the relationship was over because of something he had done, I explained it was all a part of life's lessons and reassured him my love would always be open to him. My love and acceptance provided a safe environment where he could emerge from his shell and be who he is without fear of being judged, condemned, or ridiculed. It is wonderful to watch him come to life and be happy and to know that I have been integral in his growth. In return, I am learning how to be loved without needing to protect myself in the process and not attach an expectation to it. All I have to do is relax and enjoy the wonderful experience of being loved deeply, truly, and madly.

There will never be absolute proof in this life that Russ came back as Breck to continue working on our issues together. Until I pass, I will continue to trust my intuition which tells me emphatically that he is Russ incarnate. I am eager to have all things revealed to me when I leave my body. The first thing I want is clarification about Russ and Breck. The second thing I want to know is who or what was behind the assassination of John F. Kennedy.

Now, I'm in a place of my life where I am able to let go of everything I have always wished was different about myself and instead, embrace the things that I am. For the first time, I'm experiencing what it is to love myself for who and what I am. Breck, being the evolved soul that he is, corrects me every time I am negative or self-deprecating. He has become a big part of my healing process, helping me to vibrate higher and shine as a beacon of love. As my self-love grows, my ability to accept love from others also increases. Breck showers me with his love and I readily soak it up. I have never felt more loved and cared for as I do by this man. I deserve all that he directs towards me. Our purpose of incarnating together, to facilitate healing for each other, is finally coming to fruition the second time around. What seems impossible is proving to be the perfect sequence of events to get the job done. I am so thankful Russ didn't give up on me and returned as Breck when I was finally ready to succeed at the task at hand. We are a perfect example of a soul family, agreeing to experience lifetime after lifetime and to be of service in each other's growth and evolution.

My desire to protect Breck from any insecurities about our relationship based upon my revelation of him and Russ being the same soul was needless. Breck was the one who eventually brought up his connection with Russ. One day, out of the blue, Breck shared with me that he couldn't get over how much the picture of Russ looked like him. I agreed that there was an unusually strong resemblance and I confided that I had noticed it a while back. He was curious as to why I never mentioned it. I took a deep breath and dove in. I explained who Russ was and why his picture was on the wall. I presented the evidence of why I thought there was a possibility that he might be of the same soul as Russ. Of course, the most compelling fact is that Russ passed the same year that he Breck born. Breck acknowledged what I said with an audible, "Oh" but didn't say much else. I didn't pursue it. Again, I never want Breck to think that my earlier relationship had any bearing on why I am with him. I know it is at the back of his mind though because every now and then he makes a joke about it. Ultimately, he knows our relationship is unique unto itself and is playing out just as it is meant to.

Souls incarnating on the planet are coming in at a higher vibration frequency with much more information than earlier generations. What has taken my generation decades to learn, new souls now seem to already know or are able to quickly access without much effort. As the vibrational frequency increases, the veil separating the higher dimensions is continually becoming thinner. Souls arriving on the planet now are able to access information on the other side of the veil with much more ease. They have a stronger connection with their intuition which is one of the reasons why they seem to already know higher vibrational information. It's there for the asking and they readily ask.

Breck is definitely one of those old souls that has come on to the planet retaining information gleaned from previous experiences. In one of our earlier conversations, when we were marveling at how easy it was to fall into sync with one another and be in a relationship, Breck explained to me that we are eternal and had always known each other and always will. I was surprised that he already knew that at such a young age. The concept of reincarnating lifetimes to learn and evolve was a given for him. I'm sure the tepid reaction I received when I shared my suspicion about his relationship with Russ was a result of the wisdom he already knew. It wasn't a big deal to him. In the grand scheme, it really isn't. The only thing that really matters is the eternal moment of now. This is where we are, and this is what we are learning. I think that is why the big difference in our ages has never been an issue. We stay in the moment. Our respective gifts complement each other. Between the two of us, we have everything we need to work as a team to move us forward in our lives, our spiritual growth, and our evolution. It may sound like all work and no play, but we have a lot of fun with each other in the process; making every day a joyful adventure.

My wise Breck reminded me when we first met that we are infinite. Souls, once created, never die. We reincarnate over and over again to experience the full spectrum of possibilities imaginable in order to understand what our choices are and then to choose our divinity. How can we exercise our free will to choose if we don't know what the choices are and what they entail? I mentioned earlier that reincarnation is the keystone to making the human experience work. The concept is so important that I will emphasize it again. Reincarnation makes the entire evolutionary process function perfectly in order to remember who we really are. Without it, it all falls apart. Through each lifetime, we have the opportunity and ability to create the circumstances that give us the knowledge to understand what is and what is not. The scope of it is mind boggling. When you take into consideration the full pantheon of human experience, it would be impossible to learn it in a single lifetime. Speaking from personal experience, it can take a few lifetimes to learn just one lesson. As a Pleiadian planning to incarnate at this time on Earth, I took on the genetic imprint of suicide so I could help heal it. I was told by Dr. Keith, when I broached the subject of my suicidal tendencies, that I had committed suicide, in one way or another, in the past 852 lifetimes. He gave me a minute to digest that bit of information before he added that I really needed to break the cycle this time around and finally move past it. We had a good laugh at that. So far, so good.

Historically, reincarnation was taken out of most theologies in practice today. The reason for this was that the people who ran these institutions wanted total control of their followers. They found it hard to mandate behavior and morality when the people had the option of pushing things forward into a future lifetime. In other words, "I'll do what I want now and follow the rules the next time around." For instance, reincarnation was a part of Christian teaching up until 553 A.D. At that time, the Second Council of Constantinople decided there was no place for it in the Christian Church. With reincarnation taken out of the doctrine, it was easier to instill fear in their followers and have them toe the line and do the bidding of their leaders in their one and only life. Of course, that in turn, benefitted the institution. The threat of eternal damnation proved effective in controlling behavior.

As with Breck and me, groups of souls agree to share in the process and reincarnate together, playing different roles each time for one another. The term 'soul family' has become a common phrase to help define soul agreements. In my experience with past life regression, I've learned to guide myself and others to look around and see if they recognize anybody in the life they are recalling. The answer is always yes. I love it when I meet someone for the first time and there is an instant rapport. After just a short period, sometimes only minutes, there is a feeling of comfort and familiarity that opens me right up like I've known them forever. I always joke that we must have known each other in a past life which is always met with consensus.

I absolutely love the planning pre-incarnation that obviously went into Breck and me meeting in this lifetime. We made sure on every level that we would be together. First our physical appearances were chosen perfectly to assure a physical attraction. He chose to incarnate into a family that would give him the genetics that I find irresistible: tall, muscular, swarthy, deep resonant voice, and jaw dropping masculine good looks. Given that our relationship is a May - December one, Breck gave himself an innate attraction to older men with white hair. I asked him several times in different ways about the white hair thing and he consistently answered that ever since he became sexually aware, he was drawn to men with white hair. Lucky me! On the other side of the equation, I made sure I had the genetics for everything Breck is attracted to: tall, athletic build, blue eyes and a full, thick head of white hair. I'm also amazed at the planning and logistics of ending up living in the same place. We were both born and raised in the same area of the country. Interestingly, we both ended up moving to the desert in the Southwest for the same reason, so we also share that in common. Our experiences in the desert led us both to a life in Florida. Finally, our lives had put into motion that we would both be at the same place at the same time with unusual circumstances, putting us at tables sitting next to each other. I believe all synchronistic events to be preplanned well before they ever happen. This was our destiny for sure. To cap it all off, even though we are vastly different in age, we are pretty much in the same place in our spiritual evolution. What it took me decades to remember, Breck brought with him when he incarnated. Lucky Breck!

Once again, the astrologers proved to be right. Buz said the man I dreamt of was out there but he wasn't ready for me yet. A bit of an understatement when you consider Buz said that when Breck was only five years old. I never thought I would have to wait so long to meet him. Emily said I would have my last contact with romantic love when I was 58 years old. I met Breck a couple of months before my 59th birthday. Everything seemed to point to the fact that we were each other's destiny so we made it official and got married in 2021. Our niece, Lindsey, officiated the ceremony and made it fun and memorable. I never imagined that anything like Breck and marriage was in the cards for me, but here I am a happily married man.

When we finally live enough lives to remember that we are the universal power, and that all is one, we start all over again. The circle, infinite in its geometry, has no beginning and no end. The same for a soul experience, hence the name, the circle of life. I get frustrated when I think about it. It doesn't seem fair to put in all that effort to finally reach the goal and you don't receive the time to enjoy it. From what I read, and the intuitive recognition I feel when I read it, I understand that it can be boring at the end goal. You have already done everything. There is nothing left to do except sit around and be all there is. One can only sit around and be blissed out for so long before you get bored and start longing to be a player again. The adventure of riding the roller coaster of life. The ups and downs, the twists and turns, that's where the action is!

Let me demonstrate the process by putting it into my Earthly experience of becoming spiritually evolved. I've learned to view life as a series of slopes and plateaus. Think of the plateaus in the story as lifetimes that we live. I work hard to achieve something, climbing up the side of the mountain. I arrive. It's flat as far as the eye can see. No more struggle. My accomplishment feels good and I enjoy how easy and enjoyable it makes living life. I'm coasting along for a few years thinking I've mastered everything I needed to know. Then, out of nowhere, a new challenge shows up in my life and I realize there's something more to learn. Suddenly, in front of me is another steep slope I have to start climbing if I want to continue to move forward. I do the necessary work and before I know it, I have crested onto another plateau with a new lesson learned. The feeling of accomplishment comes back and I savor it. I coast along again enjoying life and then a new challenge presents itself. The process never ends. Yes, it is great to coast on the plateau, but the real fun is in the climb. Ask any mountain climber. They take months to plan, train to get in shape, assemble equipment, and find guides who also prepare for the climb. The time arrives, they start from the bottom or base camp and slowly make the ascent. When they get to the top, they plant a flag and take a picture. They look around at the 360-degree view and realize how small the world is and that it is all one. Eventually, the thrill begins to ebb and they know it is time to descend to the bottom. The power of their achievement becomes a memory over time. Soon the desire to do it all again overtakes them and they begin to plan which mountain they are going to conquer next. It's the *getting there* that makes the blissful moment at the top all worthwhile! The love of getting there is the motivation for souls to continually come back and live lifetimes.

It is one thing to read about concepts in a book and have an intellectual understanding of them. Either you believe it or you don't. It is quite another to know you are living it. I assure everybody you are living it! If there is any doubt in your mind, find a hypnotherapist that does past life regressions. Once you experience remembering a past life, it is hard to deny that it was you having the life. Look at the people in your life as your soul family reincarnating over and over again together. What roles are you playing out for one another? What are the lessons you are teaching them? What are the lessons that they are teaching you? We are gifting everybody we encounter in the course of our daily lives with challenges and opportunities for growth. Knowing this important bit of information can change how we look at, judge, and treat other people.

I am lucky that I not only have an intuitive knowledge and understanding about reincarnation, but I also get to see it play out in my current life with my husband. Relationships can be challenging at times. That we choose to come together to assist in advancing each other on our evolutionary paths makes it easier to stay focused and committed. We understand that lives and their associated lessons are cumulative. What you glean in your present life you take with you into your next life. Hence, we are both committed to achieving as much in this life as we can so when we come together in a future life, we will be much further ahead in our evolution making our new experience together even better than what it is in this life.

I T NEVER ENDS

Transition Transform Transmutation

E arth, and the human race that inhabits it, are going through a
transition of ages that possess totally different attributes and
qualities. We are moving out of the Piscean Age and into the
Aquarian Age. The transition is gradual. It slowly started to have an
effect about 200 years before the official date of the transition with
the French and American Revolutions. It will take another 200 years
of transformation after the official date before the transition is totally
complete, with all vestiges of the Piscean Age transmutated in the
early part of the 23rd century. For our purposes here, I'm going to
give the year 1987 as the year the energy set up to confirm the
transition, the year 2012 as the debatable date of the transition, and
2044 as the year when we will be fully invested into the energy of the
Aquarian Age. I have chosen to be incarnate on the planet from start
to finish to help facilitate the transition by being a point of love and
light to balance all the dark energies that are being exposed by the
light getting brighter and brighter as the transformation slowly takes
hold.

From the year 1 A.D. to December 21, 2012 A.D. (or November
11, 2011 A.D. depending who you ask), we have been in the Piscean
Age. The energy of the Piscean Age promoted the human race to
engage in matters of the soul. The ideas of the self and connection
to a higher power consolidated in the collective consciousness. It
was the beginning of monotheistic religions in which one God was
embraced instead of many gods. The beginning of this was marked
by the chaos of the fall of the Roman Empire which provided a

ripe environment for a monotheistic ideology to flourish. In Western cultures, it is considered to be the age of Jesus Christ representing the qualities of charity, mercy, sacrifice, compassion, and forgiveness on one side and servitude, suffering, victimhood, materialism, and being controlled by a top-down power structure that told people what to do on the other side. Life's lessons in the Piscean Age on Earth were typically learned through negative experiences of pain, sacrifice, and suffering. This is what the road to heaven and eternal salvation was believed to be paved with. Interestingly, the symbols of Christianity are the same as the astrological sign Pisces: Water and the fish. Almost all wars in the past 2,000 years have been fueled in part by religion thus allowing religion to have ultimate control telling the masses what to do. Only in the past 200 years have wars begun being fought over social issues, signifying the coming Aquarian age energy.

There was a song in the 60's by the Fifth Dimension called *Aquarius - Let the Sun Shine In* that had lyrics which foretold what the astrological aspects were that would usher in the Aquarian age. Those aspects began to manifest on December 21, 2012. This is the date I use for the transition. We are now officially in the Aquarian Age. As the Piscean age slowly deconstructs with the old institutions and power structures falling apart, the qualities of the Aquarian Age are beginning to take hold. Aquarian qualities consist of democracy, freedom, humanitarianism, idealism, decentralization of power, veracity, community, philanthropy, equality, and personal power on the positive side. On the negative side are disorder, rebellion, nonconformity, impulsiveness, and detachment. Life's lessons and attainment of the divine will be gleaned through positive experiences in the Aquarian Age instead of negative ones that were experienced in the Piscean age. Whereas the Piscean age focused on spirituality, the Aquarian Age will focus on science, modernization, technology (especially computers), communication, flight, and the empowerment of the people. In my early readings, it was said repeatedly that the Aquarian Age was going to usher in the Golden Age where love, peace, and harmony would rule supreme. An age that will last 20,000 years. I can already see the glimmer of gold in the horizon!

Even though the Earth plane has been feeling the influence of the Aquarian energy for the last 250 years, the planet didn't get its first direct hit until the 1960's. People, especially the youth of the planet, came together to question, challenge, and rebel against the social and political structures that were in place for decades. People readily came together in community for the common good to protest the Vietnam war, racial inequality, and political mandates that no longer seemed just. When the power structure tried to quelch the mounting voices, riots occurred. The people refused to be pushed aside. They demanded to be heard. "Peace," became the salutation in greeting people hello or goodbye. The result was a major shift from long held beliefs causing the first cracks in government and social issues that were beginning to crumble. Unionization was empowered. Even science offered the wonders of computers, space travel, flying to the moon, and the birth control pill which freed women from the shackles of childbearing giving them dominion over their own lives. This later development ignited the age for sexual freedom and the Women's Liberation Movement and their demand for equality. Each of these changes is consistent with the qualities of the new energies of the Aquarian age.

My favorite aspect of the 60s was the counterculture. A new form of music took over the radio waves espousing peace, love, harmony, sexual freedom, change, and revolution. The Hippie movement was born that challenged the old paradigm and influenced behavior and style in culture. Social situations became less formal and more relaxed and earthy. Never was it more obvious than in the new fashion styles that became popular. Suits and dresses were replaced with wild, colorful clothing, and long hair, on both men and women, that became the new look for the younger generation. Communes explored the idea of living in a community where everybody was equal and worked for the common good. Rebellion became the catch word of the day questioning religious, family, and business values. The peace movement evolved in reaction to the Vietnam war. In 1968, one of the most historical and turbulent years in American history, I was in the third grade. I remember it as the Summer of Love that produced some amazing music. Dancing styles had drastically changed. Formal dance steps were replaced with freestyle movements which encouraged individualistic expression of the music. History books remember it as the year of assassinations, riots, and social upheaval.

I recall, one of my father's friends asked me what I wanted to be when I grew up. I proudly responded that I wanted to be a Hippie. I remember the looks on the adult faces around me registering their displeasure at my reply. It was obviously not what they were hoping to hear. I didn't care. My innate rebellious nature was ready to change the world!

The 1960s ended with two major events that happened in the summer of 1969. Aquarian energy supported innovations in flight that culminated with astronauts landing on the moon on July 20, 1969. A few weeks later, the biggest event in music history manifested in Woodstock, New York spreading a message of unity and peace. Five hundred thousand people attended for four days. It was such a loving, peaceful gathering that no incidents of violence occurred. This event typified the Aquarian energy of large groups of people coming together in peace, and harmony.

For me, growing up in the 1960s was powerful. It taught me to think, question, and analyze life in order to make good value judgments and not settle for the status quo. It instilled in me my ideals about the role of government being solely to serve the people and not to legislate morality, religion, or to propagate big business. It gave me an awareness of community and that we are all working for a common goal with nobody being better than another. It blessed me with the ability to appreciate diversity and recognize that all our gifts are unique and of value to the collective. I honor and try to protect the Earth because of the Ecology Movement that developed in response to our polluted cities. But most of all, the 60s empowered me and set me up for a lifetime of activism on every level to make change in our social and political structures, where needed. To stand in solidarity with our brothers and sisters to make the world a better place is one of the most satisfying experiences a human may have. It was a blessing to be born when I was. Not just so I could have the 60s as my foundation but to be a part of the transition into the Aquarian Age.

The 1960's were only a taste for things to come. It didn't take root because that first wave of Aquarian energy dissipated, and the global society chose to focus on other things. It wasn't until 1987 when the energies would change again to focus on the transition. It happened with the Harmonic Convergence that I discussed in an earlier chapter which opened a portal to enhance spirituality and enlightenment to the human race on the planet. I marvel that my spiritual awakening happened in 1986 which opened me up going to yoga and meeting Betty who then got me involved with Harmonic Convergence the following year. Somewhere, I believe, is a master plan for all of us. I was born at just the right time so I could be a part of the transition and to be a leader I the transformation of the human race. An old soul set in place to usher in and anchor the new energies bringing humanity a sense of community and the common good setting the stage for change on every level.

The opening of the portal also caused the magnetic grid on the planet to realign, shifting the North and South Poles to an extreme that was never measured before in core ice samplings. This realignment created new energetic dynamics on the planet. The energy shift caused an uptick in geological activities and factors into current climate change which human activity is exacerbating. Humans have a magnetic field around us and in our bodies. There is a modality called Polarity Therapy that works with opening up blocked energies and balancing and harmonizing the flow of energy in the body. Every human on the planet is affected by its magnetic grid. This energetic shift of the poles is one of the elements that is contributing to our higher vibrational frequency which is enhancing our ability to expand our conscious awareness. This opens us up to higher dimensional levels of awareness and functionality.

The first truly extraordinary event that happened after the Harmonic Convergence occurred about a year and a half later. On November 9th, 1989, the experiment of communism failed and the Berlin Wall was torn down by citizens on both sides of Germany. I remember watching live footage on the television as it happened. I was brought to tears by the sheer humanity. It was beautiful to see people climbing over the rubble from both sides of the wall and hugging each other. In the world I grew up in, it never seemed like a possibility that the borders would ever open back up and now I was witnessing just that. Suddenly, without any warning, the world was forever changed as an old dark energy disappeared from the planet and was replaced by love and enlightenment.

Three years later, in an act that was pure Aquarian, the people of Europe decided to come together and became one entity, the European Union, in order to be competitive in the world economy. The act of people joining together in community for the common good typifies the higher vibrational frequencies the planet is now working with and that are alchemizing the density into higher vibrating dimensional realms. This was all happening thanks to the Harmonic Convergence opening up the portal so planet Earth could receive and assimilate.

Unfortunately, it wasn't all good. The Earth continues to be under great stresses from the shifting energies. A magnitude 9.1 earthquake happened underneath the Indian Ocean which created a tsunami on December 26, 2004 and killed 230,000 people in 14 countries. The catastrophe generated an overwhelming and loving response from the rest of the world, who came to the aid of the survivors and their communities. Powerful earthquakes will continue to be more frequent. Destructive storms, the size of which have never been seen before, will continue to rage over the globe causing death and destruction. Global warming is melting the ice caps. These factors are facilitating souls leaving the planet because the new higher vibrations do not support the lower vibrational energy. Many of those souls are coming back immediately so they will be at a certain age and ready to create the new paradigm as the old one falls away.

These events confirm to me that the world has begun to go through a major transitional period and that it wasn't just fanciful thinking by a few overly optimistic do-gooders back in the 80's. The planet is moving from the Age of Pisces to the Aquarian Age. In my naive mind, and it seems others as well, we thought that it was all going to happen overnight like a switch being thrown. We could not have been more wrong and disappointed. It started with the Harmonic Convergence that brought in the new higher vibrational energy, but it would take 30 years to slowly begin to awaken people to the fact that society, as we knew it, needed to change. Many institutions need to disappear or evolve to serve all of humanity and not only the chosen few. True justice needs to prevail for everybody, not only to the advantage of the ruling class. Climate change has brought attention to the fact that changes in the ways of production need to happen. Governments need to be by the people and for the people and not the playthings of dictators, autocrats, and despots. Big businesses need to change from making a few rich while the rest suffer; improvements are necessary. Equitability needs to be established so everyone can share in the abundance.

November 11, 2011 brought in an amplification of the energies and accelerated the transition. The number 11 is a powerful master number which harnesses the energies of 1 and 2. The other master numbers are 22 and 33. These profound energies, when combined, embody the three stages of creation: Envisioning, creating, and sharing, respectively. The number 11 is a strong spiritual number because it enhances the qualities of spiritual intuitiveness, the visionary, and sensitivity influencing mankind. In numerology, a repeating number magnifies the power of that number. The date 11-11-11 is a repeating number and the power of it went exponential and further energized the transition into the Aquarian Age. Some people look at this date as the official turning point of the transition ushering in the new age.

The next big date was December 21, 2012. It was referred to as the end of the world and it was said that Armageddon was finally going to destroy the Earth. These predictions were based on the fact that several Mesoamerican Long Calendars ended on this date: the 13th Bak-Tun, the Mayan, and the Inca. The Eschatological beliefs said that a cataclysm would occur making way for transformative beliefs which would begin a new age. The day came and went without much fanfare, but for me it was the moment I had been waiting for my whole spiritual life. For me, the date marked the official day all the planetary aspects would be in place to usher in the Aquarian age. I couldn't help but be disappointed. I was expecting that all our institutions were going to change overnight and peace, love, and harmony would prevail. This is when I truly understood that the transition is a process taking 500 years to move from one age to the next. I embraced my commitment to stay positive and project my absolute knowing that the transition is a done deal.

There are still a lot of deconstructions of the old paradigm that need to occur before the new energies can fully take hold and give birth to a new paradigm on Earth. Since 2012, there has been a continuous breakdown of old institutions at all levels of the human experience. The old power structure knows that it is in a fight for control and is becoming more extreme in its attempts to hold its position. In doing so, they are exposing themselves for the values they really stand for. It may seem like they are winning the battle at this point because of their aggressive, desperate behavior that is constantly being reported in the media, but they are not. Much of it amounts to nothing more than propaganda. In reality, they are creating the circumstances for their own demise with their bigotry, suppression, hate, lies, and unlawful actions. Each step of the way, people have come together in community to stand against the old energy and fight for the new.

Here are some events that have happened in the past ten years that are demonstrating that the transition is happening and gaining momentum. In 2012, The Catholic church had a shocking resignation of Pope Benedict and his old conservative church dogma making way for the more progressive Pope Francis who began to transform the institution to the point that it now sanctions the blessings of gay relationships. In 2013, the Black Lives Matter movement was birthed in response to the treatment and wrongful killing of black men and women by police. It came to the forefront in 2020. The killing of George Floyd mobilized people from around the world to protest. As the needless killing of black people continues, their voices for change and justice grow louder and louder. The Women's March on January 21, 2017 was a worldwide protest of patriarchy and rhetoric threatening women's rights with millions of people participating. Not by coincidence, it occurred on the day after the inauguration of Donald Trump and was a direct response to what he represented. The Trump administration gave permission for the darkness to come out in the open by embracing white supremacy, proposing unlawful legislation to suppress the voices of anybody who dares to disagree with him and his party, and advancing the ideals of a dictatorship by denying and ignoring election results in the 2020 election. His actions gave people an opportunity to expose themselves for who and what they really were. In the beginning of 2020, the world began to shut down in response to the spread of the Covid-19 virus. This was a reset for the human race, forcing people off their proverbial hamster wheels to take time out and re-evaluate priorities. The world has not been the same since. All of these transformational changes are unavoidable and continue to accelerate with each passing year.

From a spiritual perspective this is a battle between tradition versus progress, mind versus soul, and light versus dark. As more people awaken to their divinity and power, the light they create is exposing more of the dark energies. That is why it may seem like the old paradigm and dark energies are becoming more ubiquitous and winning. As the light becomes brighter, it is illuminating the darkness, bringing it out into the open so it can be examined for what it really is. The illumination of the darkness in turn awakens more people to the light. Until now, the darkness has managed to stay hidden enabling it to continue subversive and covert power grabs. The light cannot help but to prevail.

Evidence of old energies being exposed and people's responses to them is in the news daily. The truth that has been hidden is coming forward causing bank failures, news media forced to acknowledge the misinformation they pandered, the 2020 election lies, and the attempt to hijack the presidency in the United States revealed - just to name a few. Young people are protesting around the world. Iranian women refusing to be marginalized, the French people demonstrating the loss of early retirement, the people of the European country Georgia fighting against their government's attempt to align itself with Russia, Russians refusing to be drafted into an act of aggression, and Americans in response to exploding gun violence. Global community groups are forming to serve the disenfranchised and the hungry, utilizing decentralized systems to successfully get the job done.

We live in polar realities. There has always been the Yin and the Yang, good and bad, a positive and a negative. Both experiences are important and necessary. The battel between the light and the dark energies provides an opportunity for people to make the choice between the two. When enough of us are focused on the light, the entire human race will transmute into something totally new.

I love this story about light and dark and which one will win. If you have two rooms, one filled with light and the other totally dark, with a door in between and you open the door between the two, what happens? Of course, the light will pour into the dark room illuminating it. It is impossible for it to happen any other way. The light always triumphs over the dark. Knowing this helps me to kick back and enjoy the show because I already know the outcome.

This transformation from one age into the next is all written in the stars. We are going from one astrological age to another with each representing different energies. The progression of the planets and their aspects is a blueprint for the entire transition. It kicked into full throttle in 1987 when the planets aligned to open up the portal for spiritual awakening on the planet. In 2012, the planets with their respective energies ushered in the Aquarian Age. It was predicted that the transition would take 38 years. That brings us to the present and the writing of this book. At the beginning of 2024, the planets shifted into a new era bringing the energies that will support the creation of something new to replace the old paradigm on Earth.

I believe that when the transition is complete the way we mark the passage of years will be recalibrated. The last time we transitioned from one age to the next we started to count the years from a new point. The birth of Christ became year 1 AD, Anno Domini, and everything before was noted with BC, standing for Before Christ. I believe the year 2023 is going to be year one for the new age. On March 21st, 2023, a New Moon solar eclipse (which practically happened on top of the equinox with the sun moving into Aries, the sign of new beginnings) brought in a huge flow of unconditional love and creative energies. In spiritual and astrological circles this moment in time is being referred to as the birth of the "New Earth." The term New Earth is the name given to the period on the planet when people are going to come from a place of love instead of fear. A few days later on March 23rd, Pluto, the planet of death and destruction moved into Aquarius which is going to accelerate the deconstruction of all the old institutions and power structures on Earth. Pluto went retrograde in June 2023 moving back into Capricorn supporting one last power grab for the old energies for a few months until it moves back in to Aquarius January 2024. Except for two months in the fall of 2024 Pluto will stay in Aquarius until 2044. After 2044, Pluto moves into Pisces. This is when the Aquarian Age will be free to start building the bricks and mortar of the new age. Already, all over the planet, ordinary people are coming together, refusing to continue with the old ways and are initiating a new way of doing. What takes the place of the old paradigm is going to look very different from the last 2,500 years and will be the motivation for the new timekeeping change.

My explanation of astrology regarding the transition is over simplified, truly on a kindergarten level. I highly recommend listening to some experienced astrologers explain the energy that is supporting the transition, to get a better understanding of how this is playing out and why.

Astrology is cyclical. Astrologers look at what happened the last time these planetary configurations occurred and use that to predict what will happen this time around, but astrology isn't the only factor that is playing into the transition. Our solar system is moving through a photon belt in a never before transited part of the galaxy. This is going to make the outcomes much different. This belt is bombarding our planet with a higher frequency energy that is ramping up the light. This, coupled with the astrology of the times, is awakening souls to become highly evolved humans, who are basically light beings, to manifest like never before. Also, the dark low vibrating energies can't exist in this higher frequency energy. Essentially, the light winning over the darkness is a done deal. The best thing we can do is not resist, stay emotionally detached, and enjoy the show.

There are many other events coming together at this moment that are facilitating the new age. For instance, Geoffrey Hoppe, a channeler bringing information from Adamus Saint-Germain, shared that on March 22, 2023 an event called Heaven's Cross happened. This is when the veil that separates human consciousness from the higher dimensional realms grew much thinner, making it easier for humans to have easier access to spiritual information. This will add to our ability, as the human race, to evolve to higher dimensions and raise our vibrational frequency and radiate light like never before.

Throughout 2023 and 2024, the sun is admitting solar flares in a frequency and intensity that were never seen before on the planet. Solar flares are classified according to their X-Ray brightness in wavelength range 1 – 8 angstroms. Their classifications are A, B, C, M, and X. Each one is ten times stronger than the previous classification. The last day of 2023 saw one of the strongest X Class solar flares ever recorded. This extreme solar activity will peak in 2024. Our bodies hold coding from our ancestors that has been dormant up until now. The powerful solar flares are waking these codes to make it easier for us as a race to become multidimensional.

There are many testimonials of Blue Light beings making their presence felt letting us know they are helping with our transformation into higher dimensional beings. They are intergalactics from Sirius but I like to think they from the Pleiades. Either way, they are both noted for the blue light auras. When I first heard this, I wasn't surprised. For years I saw in myself being surrounded by blue light when I meditated.

2024 is setting up to be the most tumultuous year to date in modern times. We can expect more earthquakes, volcanic eruptions, and climate disasters. Volatile energies are bringing everything to the surface at a pace that will make heads spin. Especially in April, July, and November. As things unravel on the world stage, don't revert back to fear! That is what the dark energies want. Fear keeps them empowered and in control. We need to stop repeating are old patterns. The best tools we have in our toolboxes are love, compassion, and empathy. No matter what the situation, peacefully send it love and light. Weekly global meditations times have been implemented by several sources to hold the planet in love and light as we progress through the transition. Interestingly, three of them have chosen the same time. For me it is 2:00 PM Eastern Standard Time for 15 minutes on Sundays. The flow of energy is so intense in this weekly meditation, it is almost tangible

We can use all these energies that are exposing the darkness to aid our transformation to make 2024 the most positive and productive healing year yet. When things arise in our personal lives, we need to clear them out and dissolve them so they can be transmuted into something new. When the caterpillar entombs itself in its chrysalis it goes through a complete transmutation. The caterpillar actually liquifies itself before it becomes a butterfly. Something totally different. Only through the complete destruction of the old can the new emerge.

In Chinese astrology, 2024 is the year of the Dragon. The Dragon is the only animal in the Chinese zodiac that has magical powers. It can breathe fire and fly! It is considered the luckiest year of all. How can 2024 be anything but blessed in good fortune that will bring positive change on the planet.

Be assured the light keeps getting stronger and brighter. 2025 looks like it is going to see the transition strongly taking hold with the light finally overtaking the dark. Positive change on all levels of society will be outwardly visible. Come 2026, the Aquarian Age will be in full swing with the energies of empathy, compassion, and love guiding the creation of the New Earth.

Interesting that these events are all happening so close together occurring quicker and more frequently. The inflex of energy from everything is aiding in raising our vibrational frequencies to transmute the entire human race. It's like it was all predestined!

These different energies and events are having a direct effect on the human body. It is vibrating at a higher frequency making it impossible for low vibrating diseases and organisms to afflict it. Our DNA is upgrading to support a longer lifespan and resistance to physical aging. Brain function is increasing so we may operate in the higher dimensional realms that are opening up to us. As more information comes in through the veil, our brains will then be able to process and assimilate to it. Until now, we have been operating mostly in the third dimension. Science is advancing in leaps and bounds, discovering and proving quantum physics and the existence of fractals that will help us understand and operate in higher dimensions beyond the 3D world. This will open up whole universes to us as we get in touch with our galactic roots and begin to consciously communicate with others.

Science is opening up to the idea that the human body has its own intelligence. I believe what we will be doing in the not-too-distant future, as our vibration increases, is having direct, productive conversations with our bodies to promote healing and longevity. Our bodies are continuously replacing old cells with new ones. In one year, 90% of our body's cells are replaced with new ones. Why replace the old cells with new ones that will cause disease and aging? We can tell our innate self to replace them with new, young, healthy, and viable ones that will restore our youthful, healthy, and energetic vitality. This can dramatically slow the aging process or eliminate it all together.

The transition, and the transformation that it is blessing us with, seem like they are moving at a snail's pace. In the big picture, when looking at blocks of thousands of years, a couple hundred doesn't seem like all that much. But when a life span is merely one hundred years, it can't happen quick enough. So far, transitions have to happen slowly so people can experience the changes and evolve with it. Can you imagine waking up one morning and finding a totally new government in place? Well, I can at this point, but it would probably freak a lot of other people out. How about opening up your eyes to a multilayered fractal with different aspects of your reality happening simultaneously? Without any precursor, how would you handle that without thinking you went crazy or were abducted to a different world? How about suddenly having the ability to see auras and heal people? Wouldn't that be odd and uncomfortable if it just happened overnight? Let me assure you that the transition is a done deal. Before anything can be manifested it must be supported energetically. The old energies are disappearing, and the old paradigm can't exist without them. The new energies are flooding in from every direction and they are amplifying daily. We may not see the result of them yet, but they are laying the foundation for us to create the New Earth.

We are creative beings manifesting our realities as we move forward. With the new energies of the Aquarian age, we will be creating entirely different systems, structures, and institutions. My first love was Architecture. Let me use a metaphor of developing a new building to describe the process of the transition. First, there is the planning stage; we need to construct a new building. Then comes the design phase, which is contingent on what its function is. Function then dictates how it will look. Next, a building site needs to be secured. If there is already a building on it, it needs to be torn down, but before that can happen, its current tenant must be moved out and a demolition permit procured. Once they are out, we are ready to tear down the old structure to make way for the new. Before the site can be prepped for new construction, all the necessary building permits have to be acquired. Only then can the new structure actually break ground. That is another slow process. The site has to be leveled and excavated before a foundation can be laid. After you have a solid foundation to build on, the brick-and-mortar construction can begin. I won't bore you with all of the hundreds of components that go into the actual construction, but as I am sure you can imagine, there are many. Eventually, depending on the size and complexity of the new construction, you have something new that can serve its purpose for an indefinite amount of time. In relation to the transition, we are going through now, we are just in the phase of moving out the old tenant getting ready to tear things down. It was predicted it would take 38 years from the Harmonic Convergence for all the deconstruction to be complete. That would bring us to the year 2025. I'd say we are right on target.

So far, I've related this all to global evolution, but it is happening in personal lives as well. Nobody on the planet is exempt. There isn't anyone I have talked to that hasn't gone through some big challenge leaving them and their lives changed in a dramatic way. For me, it started with a relationship that motivated me to leave my home and move across the country. Away from all my safety nets, I had to deal with a bad relationship that mirrored to me my low self-esteem. The relationship ended and I found myself in an entirely new part of the country at ground zero, trying to start my life all over again. I had lost my sense of self and my own personal power to create my reality. It took me years to see the lesson. When I finally did, I had to filter through my entire life and see how the problem originated in order to heal. It took me even longer to reclaim my personal power. It wasn't until December 2022 that everything started to fall into place and I got back into my groove of doing affirmations and opening up to healing on all levels. I feel empowered again. A sudden change in March 2023 got me writing. Something I was born to do but never felt like I was good enough to succeed at in the past. Now I sit at my computer typing away with total confidence in my ability. I continually raise my vibrational frequency as I open up to new energies, and I'm once again experiencing random epiphanies that strike when I least expect them. For example, I've recently changed my whole approach to energetic healing. For years I believed there were separate entities that came into my healing work and operated through me to heal. As my mind expanded to higher dimensions and the reality that time doesn't exist (meaning everything is happening in the eternal moment of now), I realized that those perceived separate entities are actually higher vibrational frequencies of myself. We are one with everything because everything is one. We, and all matter, are made of the same. I know that to be the Universal Divine energy that is God or source energy (or whatever name you want to attach to it). In my Earthly reality, I am facilitating the healing!

Let me see if I can sum up the multi-dimensional experience once and for all. Above the proverbial veil, is the all-knowing part of the soul that is a direct extension of Divine source. Below the veil are all the pieces of the Divine which have separated to have an incarnate experience. But they are still that one soul. They are simply fragmented into two different simultaneous experiences. When a soul chooses to do this, the piece of itself that enters the physical world becomes blind to the all-knowing piece that stays behind on the all-knowing side of the veil, with Divine source. That is how or why the term "the veil" is used. It is still there; you just can't see it. Now you have that one soul in two different places simultaneously. One part of itself is on the side of the veil that is all knowing with the Divine source and the other piece that is incarnate on the physical dimension while remaining connected. I've read that the pieces stay connected through a silver thread. The piece of the soul that stays behind with Divine source becomes the higher vibrational aspect of itself which is known as the Higher Self (and can also be thought of as the "innate" of the physical body). Other pieces can split off to become guides but they continue to be a part of the original soul which fragmented, not separate entities. In the past, before we understood the oneness of it all, we referred to them as separate entities, known as angels or other types of beings. All the split-offs on the physical side of the veil are still part of the piece that stayed on the side of the veil with the Divine source. They are all multi-dimensional aspects of the same soul and enable us to be in several places at once, in relationship to everyone else and everything simultaneously. One of the many gifts of the new age is that it will give us a definitive understanding of this and the ability to communicate between all the splits. Moving from one dimension to another while maintaining our individual sovereignty of the self within the sanctity of community and in unity with cosmic consciousness creating a powerful coherence to manifest.

I feel compelled to also point out that every soul in the universe are fractals of the divine source. This implies that we are all different facets of the Divine source, ultimately making us parts of the same whole. In more Earthly terms, you are your neighbor and your neighbor is you. That is what is meant when it is said we are one! We are in relationship with everyone and everything.

Diagram 2

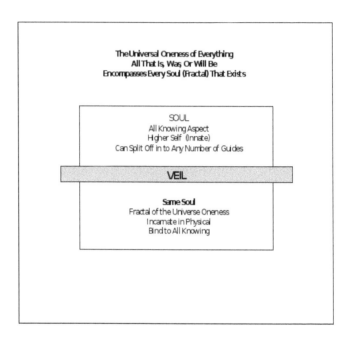

This has to be the most exciting time to be alive in human history! At first, I was frustrated that life became so hard and people and politics so ugly. Now that I understand it is part of the process of the light revealing the dark, I can embrace it for what it is and enjoy the process. I strive to not allow myself to become emotionally involved and feed the darkness but to be a point of light. Kyron is a channeled entity through Lee Carol, who was brought in at the Harmonic Convergence back in 1987, to recalibrate the magnetic grid of planet Earth and hold it during the transition. I remember listening to Kyron when I was floundering after the break up with Mr. Hollywood and I felt I had no purpose or direction. Kyron asked the question: What if your only purpose in life was to be a point of love and light on the planet to keep it in an energetic balance during the transition? I got goosebumps when I realized what the question implied. I thought yeah, I could be happy just doing that. The end result will be humanity reaching a divine connection that transcends identity, race, and social status bringing it into a new age of spiritual enlightenment. I am honored and humbled to have been blessed with such an important role. For all souls on the planet who are here at this time, you choose well. What an amazing time to be alive, witness, and participate in history in the making.

Even though the transition is a done deal, the lightworkers, old and new, and the souls just awakening should be working on raising their vibrations and being a point of love and light. Here are some suggestions as to how we can do that. First, be in love with all that we are and all that we do. We can't let yourself get caught up in the drama around us. It is not within our power to change it. Leave that to the people and institutions that are involved with the drama. We need to stay focused on our healing by facing our own fears and opening up to love without letting ourselves be caught up in other people's projections. Fear keeps us anchored in all the negative energy of the past. Try to be empathetic, but don't pity or feel sorry for others. That will just perpetuate negative energy by validating it. Send the situation love. When people try to engage you in a debate about what is right and what is wrong, we need to let go of our ego and step away. It is not our responsibility to change anybody's mind even if we could. Any negative reaction we may have will simply empower the conflict. We need to always trust in what we know to be our truth and know that everyone is doing the best that they can with what they have to work with. Send the person unconditional love to help them find their way. When observing the events around you, in your country and around the world, don't become emotional about what is happening. If we allow our emotions to run wild, it will energize whatever news event we are reacting to. Send the situation unconditional love. We always need to stay in our knowing that we are witnessing the transition in progress. We already know the outcome. Let it play out as it is meant to. Being a point of love and light to others, and every situation, is the only way to speed up the process. Without even knowing, our models for everybody around us. People always notice when we stay peaceful amongst the turmoil and will wonder why. When they ask how we are managing that, they are letting us know that they are ready to listen and hear about a new way of doing and a new way of being. This is a window of opportunity to share the knowledge that we have. In this way, we can have a positive effect and help others to awaken to who they really are and their destiny. As the number of awakened souls increases, the easier it will be for the new energies to take hold and lay the foundation for the creation of the new age.

Remembering that the only place we have any power is in our own backyards, we need to ask ourselves how we want to evolve and what we wish to manifest. When we have clear ideas, turn them into affirmations. We create everything that happens to us. It starts with a thought. Where our minds go is where our lives will go. Doing affirmations will help us be proactive in what we create by keeping your mind focused on the positive. When we say affirmations, say them as if it has already happened and we are giving thanks for having it. Having gratitude for something is key. End each manifestation with the declarative statement "I am, that I am." If we express an affirmation in desire or placing it in the future, the universe will be happy to create the experience of wanting it by not giving it to us or that it is always somewhere in our future and not your present. Apparently, the universe is very literal. If possible, do affirmations out loud. Audible words are sound vibrations. Everything in the world is made up of energy and vibrates at various frequencies. Thus, everything is a vast matrix of vibration. The vibration of the words will increase the affirmations power to manifest. Another trick my niece Lindsey, a very wise and evolved woman, shared with me is to *feel* as if the affirmation has already manifested. She presented me with the question: How would I feel if I knew somebody was giving me $3,000,000 in three days? She paused until she saw the light in my eyes. She smiled and said, "That's the feeling you need to put behind your affirmations when you are doing them." Doing affirmations will help keep our mind focused to create a positive experience of life. The confidence of our energetic intention is the engine of synchronicity that will set up the events in our lives to make it happen. Always be open to receive what you are affirming.

I wouldn't recommend doing something that I didn't believe to be effective. Let me share my personal experience with doing affirmations to validate this belief. I started doing affirmations when I was in my late twenties. I created a notebook with each page being one affirmation accompanied by a primitive picture in colored markers to represent it. I had so much fun doing it that the number of pages was always increasing. I did them out loud, once a day, three times each; one for body, one for mind, and one for spirit while I admired my artwork. Slowly the affirmations began to manifest in my everyday experience. The result was I led a wonderful, abundant life filled with health and love. Life flowed to me easily. Eventually,

I even got the relationship I was trying to attract. Mr. Hollywood represented everything I put in the affirmation that my partner would have. In retrospect, I wasn't specific enough in what I was asking for. As the relationship went south, so did my belief in affirmations. I lost the "knowing" that is key to having them work. When the relationship ended, I stopped doing affirmations altogether. I had lost my belief that they could create a positive experience by doing them because I had lost almost everything I had been affirming. My life, at this point, was not a testament to their power. When I tried to say them out loud, it just felt like a lie. I had lost that feeling of them manifesting. At the time, I didn't know enough to factor in that some things are unavoidable and are necessary for healing and evolution. Years later when my life started moving forward in positive ways, I was too lazy to restart the daily exercise of doing affirmations. With the transition in full swing and the new energies amping up in 2022, I suddenly found myself feeling very positive about the future. My higher vibrational aspect must have messaged me somehow that it was time to start doing my affirmations again. I paid attention to what I was receiving and I started doing them again that December. The difference in my life was almost instantaneous. My whole disposition changed. I was feeling more alive and positive about the present than I had in the past 15 years. My life started changing. New knowledge and information came to me every day. I knew it was important to share what I was receiving so I started writing again. I credit my daily practice of doing my affirmations with all the new and exciting changes in my life. They work! Every aspect of my life is flowing beautifully, again.

I mentioned that having gratitude is key. That is because gratitude keeps us focused on everything we already have and not on what we don't. Avoid thoughts of *want* at all costs. Replacing wanting with the joy of what we already do have will create having more. I know some people have "gratitude" friends. Somebody they connect with every day to share what they are grateful for. Other people do it at the end of the day. They look for things that happened on that day that they are grateful for. I end every day with yoga and a little meditation before I crawl into bed. When my head hits the pillow, I do my gratitude list. I always try to think of new things each night and not repeat myself. It makes me look a little deeper into my life.

The monkey mind is a wild thing, but it can be trained. Old Piscean energy has left us in the habit of looking at things negatively. To change that, we must constantly monitor our thoughts. Each time we catch ourselves thinking something negative, release the thought and consciously replace it with a positive version of the same thought; a different positive perspective. It may also be helpful to incorporate positive ways to look at things as our days play out. When we are happy doing something, we need to send out the thought "I love it when (fill in the blank). Invite positive thoughts by welcoming in an expanded consciousness of love. We need to ask the higher vibrational aspect of ourselves to activate our internal compass, quell our fears, and provide the pieces that will activate our understanding to whatever we need to know in the moment. When we ask, we receive. Always be open and ready for it to flow in. We need to talk to our innate bodies, the consciousness of the physical body, to manifest a youthful, energetic, and healthy body. It is our physical bodies that we experience the physical world through. We may as well have the best, healthy, long-lasting ones possible. All these suggestions should keep our minds pretty busy so they don't have time to slide back into the negative. I know change isn't easy, but it is worth the effort.

The most important and powerful thing we can do in the Aquarian Age is LOVE YOURSELF! Self-love will automatically open us up to our spirituality; be love, radiate love, project love onto the world. If we cannot love ourselves, we cannot truly love anyone else. We can be our own worst enemies with all our judgments and criticisms that continually flow through our monkey minds. Unfortunately, many of us were brought up to be self-deprecating. Media and advertisements make it worse with narrow definitions of beauty and perfection. Turn it off! We need to let all of that go and know that we are already perfect in our uniqueness. Accept everything that we are and have because we planned it that way before we incarnated. They are our gifts and our tools to succeed in this lifetime. Don't desire to change things we cannot change. That is just a waste of our time and energy. We are a piece of source energy, the Divine, God. If you are not loving ourselves, we are dishonoring ourselves and all of the universe.

Recognize that everybody else on the planet is made from the same energies that we are. Knowing that will make it easier to treat people as we wish to be treated. In the big picture, we are all in this together because we are all one. What we do for yourselves, we do for the collective consciousness of the planet. We are all connected. We need to be kind to ourselves and don't waste our lives doing and being something, we don't like. Find something you love to do and do that. Be happy! It is your birthright. Loving ourselves will negate any brainwashing we may have received in our lives that we were born in sin or bad by nature. How could that be possible when we are an expression of the Divine, source energy, God. Everything we are and do is holy.

The top-down power dynamic will disappear in the Aquarian Age as we recognize that we are all co-creators collaborating together to bring living-in-freedom and justice in harmony with the sovereignty of ourselves. When we get out of our minds and into our hearts, we will be living in right relationship with our bodies and planet Earth. When this transformation is complete, the stage will be set for the complete transmutation of the human race.

I was 27 years old when I participated in the Harmonic Convergence. I will be 84 years old in 2044 when Pluto moves into Pisces finalizing the deconstruction of the old Piscean Age and the Aquarius Age will be in full swing. That will be 57 years in total of being a beacon of love through some serious transitioning, transformation and transmutation. I've had a feeling my entire life that I'm going to live to be 102 years old. That would mean that I spent almost half of it seeing the transition through. What an honor! I estimate I will have twenty good years to help utilize the new Aquarian energies to help co-create something wonderful that will serve all mankind. I already have some great ideas that span the spectrum of education, ecology, economy, and government that will always honor and respect the individual with empathy and compassion, fostering unity and equality on all levels and layers. I am eager and excited to help initiate the Golden Age on Earth where everybody will live in unconditional love working for the greater good of all people on Earth. I believe, like the caterpillar and the butterfly, the human race is going through a complete transmutation. By the end of the Aquarian Age, it will be something totally different than what it has been so far.

L IQUIFY!

Prologue

N ow is the time for patience and understanding. For those that are awakened and all the souls in the process of awakening, it is time for us to be unconditional love, letting go of our judgments and expectations and hold the love and light for the souls that need a little more time to evolve into the higher vibration. The transition into the Aquarian Age is a done deal. The consciousness of the human race decided that back in 1987, when a surprisingly large number turned out for the Harmonic Convergence and opened up the planet to receiving higher consciousness energy. It has always been the decision of the human races, every step of the way. This wasn't done for us. Every moment we live is filled with infinite possibility. One decision led to another, then another. This wasn't the first chance the human race has had to evolve into higher consciousness. A few civilizations have come and gone on Earth because they weren't ready to evolve. Our present civilization could have decided on a different outcome this time too. A third world war that weaponized nuclear power and would have annihilated the human race, was definitely a possibility. Instead, the human race decided to open up the portal to a higher spiritual understanding of ourselves. The new energy is flowing in. There is no way to stop it now. The new higher vibrating energy will not support lower vibrating beings. If some souls aren't ready to evolve, they will be leaving the planet until they are. There are other worlds/planets for low vibrating beings to work out their evolution. Evolution can't be avoided. We either do it now or we do it later. We get an infinite number of chances to figure it out. It's always our choice.

The most wonderful aspect of the Aquarian age will be the end of wars on the planet. Enlightened souls will not support it. In the aftermath of war, universal love and empathy for our fellow man will facilitate great strides in healing and curing all diseases on the planet. Healthy food production will be refined in a way to feed everybody on the planet, effortlessly. All of this will be supported using funds that once went for militaries.

For those souls that are committed to the Golden Age on Earth, there is much to look forward to. Once the threat of weaponizing new technologies is gone, they will be given to the planet transforming our everyday lives. Survival will no longer consume our time and energy. A basic standard of living will be established with society providing the essentials. This will enable the populace to use a substantial amount of their time and energy to generate love and happiness to fulfill their lives. Free electricity will be considered a right, just like the air we breathe, as well as potable water as fresh as a mountain stream. Clean ways to generate energy using geothermal technology will be developed to power our homes and will be free to everybody.

Aquarian energy supports major advances in flight. Remember we flew to the moon in the 1960s. I continue to hear a lot about flying cars which should be able to land in our own front yard. This invention will change how we move about the planet. In fact, Aquarian energy supports all the sciences (which are going to explode giving birth to technologies that I can't even imagine) and will change life on Earth for the better, making everyday life easier. Communication has been expanding since the 1990s with computers and cell phones. This is going to increase exponentially, connecting every corner of the world. An understanding of the universe using quantum physics and knowledge of fractals will finally explain the multi-dimensional world we live in and give us tools to operate consciously on all levels simultaneously. I say "consciously" because we have been doing it unconsciously all along. We just didn't know it. Artificial Intelligence, or AI, is already here doing amazing things. Legislation will ensure it is regulated to serve the people in a healthy, fun, productive way, thus making it a gift to humanity. New technologies will give us the ability to see far into space to help us understand the nature of the universe. Science will prove a quantum reality that will give us an understanding of fractals and explain our complicated multidimensional realities. This new science will eventually explain and define the divine universal energy and spirituality.

From day one of the evolution of man on the planet, we have been helped covertly by beings from different worlds that are more evolved and advanced than us. Galactic's have shared their genetics and DNA to make us unique on the planet with a high brain capacity to eventually operate on multi-dimensional levels, in multi-dimensional ways, and in multi-dimensional worlds. It is my understanding that all beings in the universe are created in the image of the divine. We are all children of source, the Divine, or God. Once the threat of violence towards them is eliminated, they will show themselves and work with us hand-in-hand to guide us to evolve to their levels. This will become the norm. Don't be surprised when you meet somebody from another world, and they look just like you. Under their tutelage, the human race will advance at record speeds. The astrological energies that we are starting to receive on Earth are already supporting stronger interactions with the Galactic's. In fact, that energy is so strong presently, like the transition, it is a done deal. It may happen sooner than you think. Some say as early as 2025! Personally, I can't wait to look them in the eye and express sincere gratitude for all they have done for us. I think a big hug would be in order, too.

Communication, as well as the experience of beings from other planets, will be the key factors in creating a global community. With the availability of information, it will become impossible to hide the truth and the fear that the old power structures created will dissipate. We will finally see ourselves as equals. Nationalism will disappear. The people of the planet will become a global community defining themselves as citizens of Earth. Everybody will recognize that we are all the same, working for the same goals while honoring and embracing the diversity of individuals. Priorities will change. A desire to help each other and be of service to the community as a whole instead of being in competition for goods and services will take prevail. Resources that once went to the enrichment of the elite will be diverted into social services that will raise the living standard of all the poor and disadvantaged. No longer will homelessness be an issue. Jobs with generous compensations will be created in new peacetime endeavors that will employ all. Each individual will find their perfect fit which makes them happy and fulfilled. The idea of going to work will no longer be a negative. It will be a joyful experience that people will look forward to. All professions will be seen as being vital to the success of the whole and valued the same.

Amazing advances in medicine and the healing arts will include direct conscious communication with the body and vibrational healing. These will replace the barbaric drugging and cutting into the body that we do now. As people evolve into their own power and learn to function in a multi-dimensional world, their ability to communicate with their bodies and create perfect, disease-free homeostasis will be the norm. This will reduce the body's vulnerability to disease. For medical issues that cannot be controlled by the power of the mind, resources now available will be directed towards research to help the sciences discover new ways to heal the body using physics. We already know that everything is a vibration, including our bodies. Vibrational healing will become state of the art. Everyone will have the same universal health care, if needed. Pain and suffering, due to issues with the body, will be eliminated.

Producing a sustainable healthy food supply will be the biggest industry on the planet. Surplus monies will be utilized to develop healthier, natural, nutrient rich foods that will thrive in the depleted soils. Water for agriculture and human consumption will be plentiful due to new and easy ways to desalinate water using magnetic technology. The produce that these new technologies provide will be available to everyone equally. These new developments will end hunger and starvation on the planet.

The new Aquarian energy is opening us up to a stronger sense of community where everybody is equally important. An intrinsic love for ourselves and our fellow man will ensure that all the new advances that are coming our way will be utilized for the people and their general wellbeing with all profiting equally. I'm sure you have experienced the joy and satisfaction that settles in after you have done a good deed for somebody else. Now imagine a lifetime of feeling like that taking you to new levels of consciousness you have never experienced before. I've been told that, as humans, it is impossible to fathom the depth of emotion which is generated by experiencing the Divine. I think that will change.

I began the chapter entitled Setting Intentions sharing my three wishes. They are: An end to all wars, a cure for all disease, and the end to world hunger. I am ecstatic to know they will all be coming true in the Aquarian age because of the philanthropy of each individual towards their fellow man. The end of needless pain and suffering will be big strides in moving to a more utopian society on the planet. I know that humans and life on the planet will never be perfect, but we will be eons ahead of where we are now. My early fantasy of how life on the planet could be will become a reality. I cannot seem to find the words - yet - to express how the thought of this makes me feel.

I want to assure everybody that it's not too late for us to experience and reap the benefits of our efforts to assist in manifesting this new age. Not only will we enjoy the process of ushering in the Aquarian age, but we will be able to experience all our efforts to transition in our next lives. We will continue to reincarnate, but now, with the new energies, we will be retaining much more information from our previous lives making our new lives easier, healthier, and richer. When this life is over, it won't take long for us to plan something new and get back in the saddle and ride into a new adventure in the physical world.

The Golden Age that I have been reading about throughout my life is upon us. I never thought I would see the day, but here it is. Love, peace, and harmony will guide the human race to new levels of evolution bringing us closer to our divinity. My path in this lifetime has brought me to this point. It's been an interesting ride. A ride I never could have imagined. My stories are everybody's stories. I had fun putting them down on paper. I hope sharing them here will help other people open up to their own paths. Life may seem random, but it's not. It has a purpose. We are here to open up to and experience our divinity. In doing so, we will help each and every soul on the planet to do the same. We are all in this together. What we do for ourselves we do for the collective consciousness of the planet.

I invite everybody to share their stories with friends and family. You never know what effect they may have in someone's life. Feel free to send them to me, also. I would be interested to hear about your journeys. Who knows, they can make for an interesting compilation book in the future.

WE GOT THIS!!!

ACKNOWLEDGEMENTS

I would like to thank all my family and friends who jumped on the band wagon when I finally decided to pursue my dream of sharing my spiritual evolution with the world in order to help others along on their own spiritual journeys. Your enthusiasm and support buoyed me through my process and helped me bring this book to its natural conclusion.

I want to especially bless and applaud Lindsey Jean Sykora in unwittingly offering to edit the manuscript. She had no idea what she was getting into. She offered her wisdom and perceptions along the way as she made sure my spelling and grammar was spot on. Thank you so much for your patience and determination. I would also like to give a nod to Joyce Hinckle who also offered her expertise in grammar and punctuation.

I have to commend my spiritual soul sisters who bravely agreed to read the unfinished manuscript and, with courage and honesty, critique it. Not an easy thing to do when you don't want to offend someone you love. Each was unique and invaluable in what they offered. Let me do this in alphabetical order: Patricia Leigh Allen challenged me to explain anything that might have left a question mark in the readers mind especially when it came to sequence of events and geography, Jane E. Fletcher-Ortman confirmed the importance of the book and the need to get it published ASAP, Penelope Levario gifted me with her creative writing expertise and encouraged me to flush out situations and characters making the stories much richer, Dr. Sandra Marie Robinson who went down this road before me and offered her experience, insights, and know how at the drop of a hat, and Sylvia Low Tiffany who painstakingly did all of the above and researched information to see where it needed to be clarified, My love and appreciation to all of you. Without each of you, *Escaping Madness* would not be the book that it is today.

I know that we are all healers helping each other along in our growth and evolution, but I think it is important to honor all the people I worked with over the years that inspired me to evolve into a Medical Intuitive. Unfortunately, many of their names elude be, but here are the ones I could never forget: Mary Lou Schroeder, Dr. Keith Jordan, and Sarah Stark.

I also want to thank Delia Skye who took me to lunch one day and taught my much about getting a book published and bolstered my courage to put myself out there.

Finally, I want to give my handsome husband Breck a standing ovation for his unflagging support while I wrote. He took over all the daily responsibilities of living life, freeing my time up to write. Thanks for not fighting me too much for computer time.

Bibliography

Chbosky, Stephen, *The Perks of Being a Wallflower.* Simon & Schuster, 1999

Hay, Louise, *You Can Heal Your Life.* Hay House, Inc, 1984

MacLaine, Shirley, *Out on a Limb.* Bantam, 1983

Redfield, James, *The Celestine Prophecy.* Satori Publishing, 1993

Tolle, Eckhart, *A New Earth.* First Plume Printing, 2005

von Danikien, Erich, *The Chariots of the Gods.* Bantam, 1971

About the Author

Mark Robinson has devoted his life to learning, understanding, and expanding what it is to be a spiritual being incarnated in a physical body in this age of transition on planet Earth. Blessed with charm and charisma, people have always been drawn to him. As a successful yoga instructor and massage therapist, he worked as a consultant with the business community training personnel teams in relaxation and ways to stay young and healthy. Over the years, he has expanded and honed his abilities as an energetic healer and medical intuitive, becoming an authority sought after for workshops, featured presenter at seminars, and guest host for various podcasts.

Mark is well traveled and has been an active, global presence and voice of the awakening that is in progress. He has always been a facilitator for helping others escape their spiritual closets and embrace their unique, energetic selves and oneness with the universe. In his first book, Mark has delved deep into his conscious memories and intuitive self with courage and honesty to chronicle his life experiences in his slice-of-spiritual-life memoir. It is aimed at helping all awakening souls, new and old, understand and assimilate what they are experiencing. Wherever Mark goes, he is a passionate, fresh voice for the transition into the New Earth!

Mark was amazed to learn how his personal astrology creates a blueprint for him to be a highly effective communicator and successful writer. Not only does he have Gemini, the sign of communication, on his Midheaven, which governs his career, but he has Mercury in Leo, the most creative sign, in the 12th house. This is the best placement of Mercury possible for anybody who wants to excel as a writer! Mark's astrology explains his intrinsic love for the written word and his ability to be an excellent wordsmith in any medium. Interestingly, according to the Mayan astrological system, Dreamspell, he was born on the auspicious day of Day Out of Time which is the galactic archetype of The Profit. As a Red Skywalker, Mark is living his destiny, continuing on his path of service with *Escaping Madness* to propel each of us and all of humankind into the Golden Age.

Read more at endeavortoevolve.com.

About the Publisher

Staman publishing was established to convey the message from the gallatics that embodies the New Earth that is taking shape in the Aquarian Age mankind is now living in.

Read more at endeavortoevolve.com.

Milton Keynes UK
Ingram Content Group UK Ltd.
UKHW012321110424
440929UK00001B/51